A STORY UNTOLD

A STORY UNTOLD

Black Men & Women in Athens History

MICHAEL L. THURMOND

Published by Deeds Publishing in Athens, GA
www.deedspublishing.com

Printed in The United States of America

Library of Congress Cataloging-in-Publications data is available upon request.

978-1-947309-66-1

Books are available in quantity for promotional or premium use. For information, email info@deedspublishing.com.

Third Edition, 2019

10 9 8 7 6 5 4 3 2 1

SPECIAL TRIBUTE TO SPONSORS

This third edition of *A Story Untold: Black Men and Women in Athens History*, was made possible through the generous contributions of:

Dr. and Mrs. Farris T. Johnson, Jr.
WXAG Radio Station
"The Heart & Soul of Athens, GA"

This work is dedicated to
my father and mother,
Sidney and Vanilla Thurmond

Contents

Introduction to the Third Edition

Athens Historical Society

Athens Historical Society ("AHS"), in conjunction with Deeds Publishing, Athens, Georgia, is pleased to present this third edition of A Story Untold, Black Men and Women in Athens History, by Michael L. Thurmond. This project began in March 2018, when it was brought to the AHS board's attention that 2018 marked the 40th anniversary of the publication of A Story Untold. The book had been out of print since the early 2000s and publication of a third edition was a natural project for AHS to undertake.

After a summer of collaborative effort on the part of Mike Thurmond, AHS and Deeds Publishing, it was time to announce the project publicly. In a presentation co-sponsored by the Athens-Clarke County Library Heritage Room, on October 21, 2018, the new cover of the third edition was unveiled and Thurmond addressed an overflow crowd gathered in the Appleton Auditorium of the Athens-Clarke County Public Library. In his presentation that afternoon, described by a long-time member of AHS as the best AHS program ever, Thurmond chronicled the perfect introduction to his book.

"*A Story Untold* was born in a classroom in Clarke Central High School in 1971," Thurmond began. That was the year school consolidation was implemented in Clarke County. The all-black Burney-Harris High School merged into the predominantly-white Athens High School, which was renamed Clarke Central High School. An 18-year-old Thurmond was a member of the first graduating class and served as co-president of the student council. One of his teachers that year was renowned educator Elizabeth King, who taught black history. Thurmond recalled that Miss King's class was the only class in the school that did not have a textbook. She searched for and printed articles from prominent black publications that she handed out to her students as a substitute for the lack of a textbook. Thurmond was appalled by this this situation and complained to the administration that the school system was discriminating against her class. Thurmond recalled, "Miss King said, 'If you want a textbook, why don't you go write one.' I walked out of that classroom inspired and determined to one day write a book about black history."

After graduating from high school, Thurmond furthered his education at Paine College, Augusta, and then at the University of South Carolina School of Law. As his education continued so did the pull he felt to write about black history.

There was a Sunday tradition in the Thurmond family. After church, his parents and siblings would sit around the kitchen table and discuss politics and world events. Being the youngest member of the family, Thurmond said he had to earn the right to participate in the debates. One particular Sunday the debate was about the historical relevance of black Athenians. The family was divided on this issue—some believing black Athenians already held a place in history, while others thought the black community's history was unknown and unrecognized. The debate piqued Thurmond's curiosity and after dinner he went to the Special Collections Library at the University of Georgia to see if its vast collection included any history on the African American community in Athens. After a lengthy search, Thurmond had become discouraged over not being able to find any history about Athens's black community. He was about to give up and head home when he found a master thesis about Athens during the Antebellum period. "I was sitting in the Hargrett special collections section of UGA's main library with tears streaming from my eyes," he recalled, still feeling the emotion of that long-ago evening.

Thurmond initiated his effort to document the history of the black community during the summer between college and the start of law school. He conceived an idea of creating a pamphlet on the African American history of Athens to be provided to local schools. He shared the idea with then Superintend of Schools in Clarke County, Dr. Charles McDaniel. McDaniel agreed to pay Thurmond $400 to create the pamphlet and gave him four weeks to finish the project. Thurmond completed the project on schedule and then left for law school.

Unveiling of Book Cover. Athens-Clarke County Public Library, October 21, 2018, Michael L. Thurmond (left) and Dan A; Aldridge, Jr. (right)

At that point in his life, Thurmond confided, writing the history of black men and women in the Athens community was part of his being and he was not to be denied. Thurmond added, smiling broadly, "The fire had been lit."

On his first break from law school, he continued his research. Balancing the strenuous demands of law school and research on Athens's black community, over the ensuing years *A Story Untold* emerged and was published in 1978.

As the sun began to set over the Athens-Clarke County Library, Thurmond scanned the audience—young and old, black and white—and concluded:

"We recognize that black history is American history. People of all races and colors understand that defining, documenting and sharing our history benefits all of us. As Southerners, we are connected by a shared heritage and history."."

With the publication of this third edition, *A Story Untold* will reach a new generation and continue to be an inspiration to generations to come. Thurmond is owed a debt of gratitude for authoring this work, which has brought to light and preserved the contributions to the history of our community and state of the individuals chronicled in the pages that follow. Athens Historical Society is proud to have played a role in making this possible.

—Dan A. Aldridge, Jr.
Athens Historical Society, Board
February 2019

Author's Foreword to the First Edition

This book is a compilation of nine written essays and one pictorial essay concerning the history of black men and women in Athens, Georgia. Each essay depicts either an individual contribution or the historical development of one of the major institutions within the Athens black community.

Although the original publishing agreement required only a "page and a half of typewritten material for each section," it was discovered that this would be impossible. In fact, what began as only a trickle of information soon erupted into a flood tide of facts, dates, and events concerning the history of African American Athenians.

Despite the expanded scope of this work, the reader should not fall victim to the false assumption that it adequately covers the subject about which it is written. It does not. Too much has escaped detection. Far too much remains to be written. Hopefully, what is written will not quench but will increase the reader's thirst for knowledge of the black man's contributions to the growth and progress of our city, state, and nation.

My principal hope is that the young people who read this material will become more knowledgeable about their past. Subsequently, they may better understand their present, which will ultimately enhance their acquisition of a more glorious future.

***

This book represents the culmination of the efforts and sacrifices of many people. They represent, more or less, the entire spectrum of racial, ethnic, social, and political persuasions within the greater Athens community. Although it would be impossible to list all of these individuals, there are some who merit special consideration and attention.

First, I would like to express my love and appreciation to my brothers and sisters, Jewell, Sidney Mae, Joe, Charles, Swanson, James, Vera, and "Cat." They have been a constant source of encouragement throughout my life. In addition, my friends Neva Joyce Mayweather and Fred O. Smith spent many hours helping to research material for this book.

Special appreciation is also due to Dorothy Sparer, my editor; Don Smith, designer of the book; Lisa Rankin, compositor; and Julie Jennison, proofreader. These people joined in this labor of love with vim and vigor.

Publication of this book would not have been possible without the interest and confidence shown by Charles McDaniel, Don Hight, Frusanna Booth, and Farris Johnson, Sr.

Thanks also to Dr. Charles Wynes for checking the historical accuracy of parts of the book, and to others who helped: Rosa Strickland, Laura Livingston, Eva Howard, Harry "Squab" Jones, Sampson Edwards, Alice Wimberly, Conoly Hester, Frances Smith, Maude Morton, H.T. Edwards, Sr., Beadie C. Alexander, Annie R. Thomas, the Rev. Maurice Cherry, Joan Humphries, Carolyn Weaver, Rowena McCoy, Cheryl Walker, Clara Gay, Hortense Shelton, Carol Young, H.T. Allen, Mary Trawick, LaGrange DuPree, Joe Taylor, Mary Lizzie Green, Grace Barnett, and the many helpful people at Paine College.

—Michael L. Thurmond
Athens, Georgia 1978

Editor's Bicentennial Update

Second Edition, 2001

The reprinting of *A Story Untold* is a fitting project for the observance of the 200th anniversary of the founding of Athens and Clarke County. This is a truly important work, pulling together in one place the astounding story of the African-American community in Athens from the end of slavery through the modern civil rights era.

It is a story that by 1978, when the book was first printed, had largely been forgotten (hence, the title) the story of freed slaves who created churches, schools, businesses, lodges, and— against great obstacles—a professional middle class of doctors, lawyers, politicians, journalists, musicians and educators.

They built the first black high school in the state to be fully accredited. They constructed professional buildings, opera houses and hospitals. They were early innovators in vocational education. They founded colleges, and introduced the country to the music of their slave grandparents.

In the 1970s, this glorious history was largely hidden in the yellowed scrapbooks of a few long-time residents and in the dusty stacks of the University of Georgia Hargrett Library. During and after The Great Depression, much of the black middle class had moved to other areas in search of greater and more equal opportunity. Urban Renewal, economic progress, and benign neglect had destroyed many historic landmarks.

New people moved to Athens or were born here who knew little of the community's past.

Michael Thurmond's book pulled this material together and made us all aware of it—invigorating the black community and generating white respect. The book invigorated the African American preservation movement in Clarke County. It influenced later general histories of the area by James Reap, Frances Thomas and myself—quietly ending decades of historical neglect.

The first publisher of *A Story Untold* was the Clarke County Board of Education, which placed copies of this well-researched collection of essays in the schools so young people, white and black, could learn of these early achievements. Now local educators will once again have access to this valuable resource.

This special Bicentennial edition is updated and newly indexed. It includes the integrated face of today's Athens, as well as historical information not available at the time of the first edition. It documents a growing appreciation for the historic contributions of the past and for the leadership abilities of a new generation of black Athenians. The author rewrote the chapter on Samuel Harris, one of his personal heroes, to add additional details not available when the book was first published.

Since 1978, the Susan Medical Building has been renovated by Thurmond and Chestnut Grove Baptist Church has completed the restoration of a one-room county school on its grounds. The 1914 Athens High and Industrial School building on Reese Street was restored in 1998 by the Athens Masonic Association with local government support. First African Methodist Episcopal (A.M.E.) Church has restored the home of long-time member Dr. Ida Johnson Hiram, and the four-story Morton Building is preserved and renovated as a community performing arts center.

National Register of Historic Places listings for Athens include the Morton, First A.M.E. Church, Chestnut Grove School, Reese Street and West Hancock Avenue historic districts, (containing the Susan Medical Center and the Hiram Home), and Rock-springs Shotgun Row. Markers on the University of Georgia campus commemorate the integration of the school and the former site of Jeruel Academy/Union Baptist Institute. Alumni and preservation associations have formed for Athens High and Industrial and for Jeruel/Union.

—Conoly Hester, editor
Athens, Georgia 2001

THEY SHAPED ATHENS HISTORY

1865: JUBILEE DAY!

The end of slavery for 5,000 blacks in Athens and Clarke County comes on the morning of May 4.

1866: PIERCE'S CHAPEL A.M.E. CHURCH (renamed First A.M.E.)

The first black church in Athens opens its doors.

1868: ALFRED RICHARDSON AND MADISON DAVIS

The first of their race to be elected to the Georgia State Legislature from Clarke County.

1868: KNOX INSTITUTE

The first school for blacks in Athens opens its doors.

1873: LUCIUS HENRY HOLSEY

Rises from the depths of illiteracy and slavery to become at the age of thirty, "one of the youngest men ever elected bishop in any age or church."

1879: W. H. HEARD and W. A. PLEDGER

Publish the *Athens Blade*, Athens's first black newspaper.

1883: MADISON DAVIS

A former slave becomes the first black man to be appointed postmaster in Athens.

1888: HALL JOHNSON

World-famous composer, conductor, and arranger is born in Athens.

1891: WASHINGTON W. KING

A member of a prominent family of three generations of builders, designed and built the covered bridge that spanned the North Oconee River on College Avenue, connecting downtown Athens with rural farm areas on the other side. In 1965, the bridge was disassembled and moved to its present location in Stone Mountain State Park.

1901: DR. B. B. S. THOMPSON

Athens's first black woman physician opens her office.

1910: IDA MAE HIRAM

Passes the Georgia Dental Board exams in 1910, becoming the first black woman dentist in the state. She will practice in Athens for the next fifty-five years.

1931: JULLIETTE DERRICOTTE

Internationally known YWCA organizer and college educator, dies when she is refused admission to a Dalton hospital following an automobile accident.

1946: DR. ANDREW JONES

Opens first black maternity hospital in the Susan Building.

1955: C. H. LYONS, SR.

Principal of Union Baptist Institute and outstanding educator, he is the first black man to have a school in Clarke County named in his honor.

1961: CHARLAYNE HUNTER AND HAMILTON HOLMES

The first black students to be admitted to the University of Georgia.

1961: ARCHIBALD KILLIAN AND DONALD MOON

Hired as the first African Americans in the Athens Police Department.

1963: WILUCIA GREEN, MARGIE GREEN, AGNES GREEN, BONNIE HAMPTON, AND SCOTT KILLIAN

The first black children to attend the previously all-white schools in Clarke County, in September.

1968: WILBUR P. JONES AND JOHN E. TAYLOR

The first blacks to be appointed to the Clarke County Board of Education.

1970: ED TURNER

Elected Athens's first black city councilman.

1988: MIRIAM MOORE

First black woman elected to city council.

1986: MICHAEL THURMOND

Becomes first black elected to the Georgia General Assembly from Clarke County since Reconstruction.

1995: VERNON PAYNE

Becomes first black elected chairman of the Clarke County Board of Education.

1995: JUDGE STEVE JONES

Athenian appointed county's first black superior court judge November 17, and elected to full term in 1996. Judge Jones previously served as first black judge of Athens Municipal Court. In 2011 he was appointed by President Barak Obama to a federal judgeship on the United States District Court for the Northern District of Georgia.

1997: JOSEPH H. "JACK" LUMPKIN, SR.

The first African-American Chief of Police is named Jan. 1; an Athens native with 22 years' experience in local department and five years as police chief in Toccoa and Albany.

1997: BARBARA ARCHIBALD

First African-American Athenian appointed to the State Board of Education.

1999: HARRIET POWERS

A quilt she made in the nineteenth-century holds an honored position in Atlanta History Center southern quilt exhibition in April; the first time one of her quilts has been shown in Georgia in more than a century.

2001: IRA EDWARDS

Becomes Clarke County's first black sheriff on January 1.

JUBILEE!

See these poor souls from Africa
Transported to America;
We are stolen, and sold in Georgia,
Will you go along with me?
We are stolen, and sold in Georgia,
Come sound the jubilee!

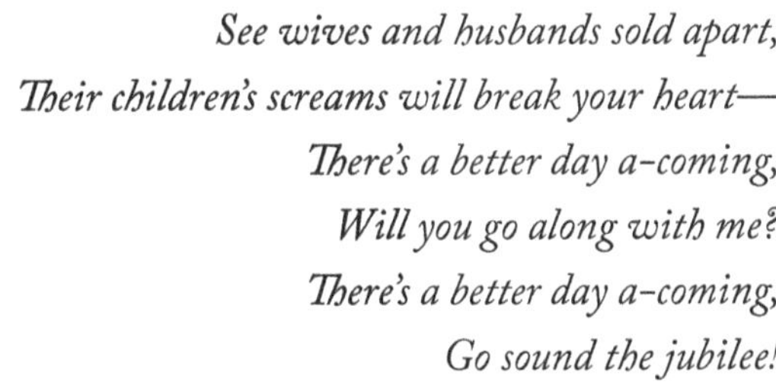

See wives and husbands sold apart,
Their children's screams will break your heart—
There's a better day a-coming,
Will you go along with me?
There's a better day a-coming,
Go sound the jubilee!

W. W. Brown
slave narrative

JUBILEE! IT WAS A DAY OF DAYS.

Jubilee! It was the event that marked the end of decades of deprivation and human slavery.

Jubilee! It was the nightfall of misery and the breaking dawn of a day of freedom.

Jubilee! It was running from the cotton fields shouting, "Free at last! Free at last!"

Jubilee! It was a time to laugh and a time to cry.

Jubilee! It was a time of divine redemption and the answer to millions of prayers. To some it was the "literal coming of the Lord."

Historian Lerone Bennett wrote, "It was the turning of worlds, the apocalyptic ending of centuries of bondage, the fulfillment of the exigencies of history and the prophecy of the Lord."

Some seventy years after the event, W.E.B. Dubois described the Jubilee as the "Golden Dawn." "It was," he said, "all foolish, bizarre, and tawdry. Gangs of dirty Negroes howling and dancing ... mistaking war, destruction and revolution for the mystery of the free human soul...."

To abolitionist Frederick Douglass who witnessed it, the Jubilee was "one of the major events of the nineteenth century and a down payment on the redemption of the American soul." According to Felix Heywood, freedom had come suddenly and unexpectedly. "Halleluyah broke out ... We was free. Just like that, we was free."

"It was a time of times, and a half time," wrote Henry McNeal Turner, a black clergyman who would later preach to integrated audiences in Athens. After witnessing scenes "that made the nerves quiver," he predicted that "nothing like it will ever be seen again in this life."

The concept of the Jubilee was probably born in the secret brush arbor religious meetings of the American slaves. It represented the transformation of an Old Testament Hebrew law that required the emancipation of all slaves and the restoration of all conquered land to the original owners every fifty years. This was interpreted to mean that the God of history would intervene on behalf of the oppressed and deliver them from the oppressors. For many black slaves, the Jubilee was the actual coming of the Kingdom of God.

But it must be remembered that the "day of freedom" came at different times and in different ways to four million American slaves. In fact, the Jubilee may be more correctly categorized as the beginning of a process rather than the occurrence of a single event. And the process of liberation that began with the Jubilee continues even today.

In Athens, Georgia, the day of Jubilee arrived around 10 a.m. on May 4, 1865, when a group of Union cavalrymen rode into the streets of the city. Although the official emancipation decree was not issued until May 15, the inhabitants of Athens, both black and white, knew that the South and its peculiar institution had fallen. The nearly five thousand slaves in Athens and Clarke County quickly realized that the chains of slavery had been broken.

"I was standing on the corner of Jackson Street when they said freedom had come." Tom Singleton, an Athens slave who served two years in the Confederate army, remembered the morning when the Yankees rode into Athens. "That sure was a rally day for the blacks," Singleton said. "About a thousand in all were standing around here in Athens that day."

Young Annie White (later, Mrs. P.H. Mell), who was in the middle of her morning lessons at Lucy Cobb Institute, a finishing school for privileged young white girls, was distracted by some commotion in the streets. Although it was against the rules, she ran to the windows with the other students and saw "to our utter horror the street in front of the Lucy Cobb was full of bluecoats. I will never forget my terror," she wrote years later. Classes were immediately dismissed and the students were instructed to go directly home.

And for good reason. The Union troops had come to Athens in search of Jefferson Davis, the president of a crumbling Confederacy, who fled into the countryside. Unable to find Davis, the soldiers spent their idle hours plundering the defenseless city. Athens became the scene of chaos and mixed emotions.

Fearing for their lives and property, white Athenians desperately attempted to hide their most valuable possessions and to protect themselves from the rampaging soldiers. Local blacks, who in the span of only a few minutes had crossed the 250-year-old chasm between slavery and freedom, simply jubileed in the streets.

Another group of blacks gathered in front of the Athens Town Hall to erect a "liberty flag pole." A United States flag was hoisted to the top of the staff while the former slaves laughed and danced around the pole shouting, "We rally around the flag pole of liberty. The Union forever, Hurrah! Boys Hurrah!"

A semblance of order was finally restored in the city when General William J. Palmer, the Union commander, arrived on the scene a few hours later. Two days later Captain A.B. Cree of Iowa became the first of three Union officers to take permanent military charge of postbellum Athens. The occupation troops were quartered in the deserted buildings on the campus of the University of Georgia. The lone exception was the university library "where Chancellor Lipscomb was allowed to stand watch."

As word of the soldiers' arrival spread by way of the slave grapevine, "hundreds of dusky field hands flocked into Athens to greet their liberators and to taste the heady wine of freedom." Susan Castle, a slave on a rural plantation, remembered that emotional moment.

> Some of the slaves shouted and hollered for joy when Miss Marion called us together and said us was free and wasn't slaves no more. Most of them went right out and left her and hired out to make money for themselves.

Prominent Athenian Dr. Henry Hull, seeing the proverbial handwriting on the wall, called up the slaves from his plantation in the country and told them that they were free. No doubt this particular drama was reenacted hundreds of times throughout the South as the yoke of slavery was lifted from the shoulders of the black race.

Of the sixteen house servants at the Thomas Street residence of Dr. Hull, the nurse and her family went to another part of town. The seamstress and her daughters moved into a small house owned by their former master and eventually became self-supporting. And the Hulls' carriage driver went to work for a livery stable.

Many freedmen tried to be independent farmers. Augustus Longstreet Hull's father, Dr. Henry Hull, was visited by one of his former bondsmen not long after the emancipation of the Athens slaves. The man wanted to buy a parcel of land, and the younger Hull described the transaction in his *Annals of Athens*.

> He took out a little bag and emptied on the table fifty dollars or more in every conceivable coin that would pass. There were Mexican dollars and Spanish dollars, thrips and dimes, sixpence and copper cents, ha'pennies and quarters. He had been saving them for years, doubtless with a vague idea of some day buying his freedom.

Local newspaper editor John Christy, a staunch supporter of slavery and the Southern war effort, editorially acquiesced to the forces of change.

> From the lights before us, it seems to be the determination of the Federal Government to compel us to abandon that cherished institution.... Submit cheerfully.... Let there be no unmanly repining.

However, it must be noted that the climactic arrival of emancipation produced varied and sometimes contradictory reactions among the freedmen of northeast Georgia. Many blacks chose to remain on their former masters' plantations, possibly because their conceptions of loyalty were stronger than the lure of self-sufficiency, or because they simply had nowhere else to go.

Many of their former owners offered to pay the freedmen wages in reward for their continued services. Joe Echols of Oglethorpe County was such a man. Robert Sheperd, one of his former slaves, recalled:

> He said he would pay us for our work, and take care of us if us stayed or, if us wanted to work on shares, he would allow us to work some land that way. A few of the folks drifted off, but most of them stayed right thar till they died.

On other plantations, Jubilee assumed the form of ecstatic celebrations accompanied by the seizure and destruction of the slave masters' property. Encouraged by the much-rumored prospect of having their former owners' property ultimately divided among them, Athens freedmen began to take food, clothing, livestock and other valuables. These seizures continued and increased throughout the remainder of 1865, even though the city was placed under the permanent occupation of federal troops in May of that year.

White Athenians became totally incensed with the continual succession of storehouse burglaries, and openly accused the occupation troops of negligence in the maintenance of law and order in the city. Although the Northern troops were somewhat less than diligent in their law enforcement efforts, they were not totally indifferent to the plight of local whites.

In response to pressure, the bluecoats arrested 150 blacks for stealing during one seven-day period. Historian Augustus Hull described some of the penalties meted out to these so-called suspects by the provost marshal, who simply assumed they were guilty.

> Some were tied up by the thumbs standing tiptoe. One young Negro, a well-known character, Mose Rumney by name, was taken and one side

> of his head shaven clean from the middle down, the wool being left untouched on the other side. A barrel with sleeve holes cut in it was slipped over his head, and on it the words "I am a thief" plainly painted.

Rumney and another black youth were then marched through the streets of Athens "with a fife and drum to the tune of the 'Rogues March,'" followed by a laughing crowd of soldiers, boys, and other blacks.

There is at least one recorded incident of a black rebellion against the vigilante tactics of the whites. On the night of July 10, Sheriff W.Y. Elder's posse was out looking for the men who had stolen some livestock on the outskirts of Athens. They seized thirty blacks and were about to take them to jail, when suddenly they were attacked by a group of freedmen who routed the posse and set the prisoners free.

After the initial jubilation of emancipation had subsided, many of the slaves who had inhabited the rural plantations began to migrate to urban areas in ever greater numbers. Throughout the summer and fall of 1865, Athens was the focal point of black migration in northeast Georgia.

"Right off colored folks started on the move," one former slave recalled. "They seemed to want to get closer to freedom, so they'd know what it was—like it was a place or a city." John Eaton, a Union officer who witnessed this mass movement on southern roads, wrote:

> Imagine if you will a slave population... rising up and leaving its ancient bondage, forsaking its local traditions and all the associations and attractions of the old plantation life, coming garbed in rags or in silks, with feet shod or bleeding, individually or in families and in larger groups.

By the end of the year Athens was simply overflowing with freedmen. The *Southern Banner*, a local white newspaper, lashed out at what was apparently a rapidly growing number of blacks in the city: "Can anybody tell where so many idle Negroes come from? Like the frogs of Egypt, they seem to be everywhere and in everybody's way."

The influx of blacks into the city created a critical housing shortage. This problem was complicated by the fact that white landowners were reluctant to rent to the penniless and jobless freedmen. In the words of Frederick Douglass, the slaves had been set free—"free to the wind, free to the rain, free to suffering and want, free to the wrath of their former masters. They had no land, they had no tools, they had no capital...."

This situation forced black migrants in Athens to congregate in settlements of hastily built shanties on the outskirts of the city. The migrants were joined by Athens freedmen who preferred freedom to the relative confinement of the servants' quarters behind the Big House. Whites dubbed the largest of these ghettos, on the eastern bank of the Oconee River, "Blackfriars" in mocking comparison to the fashionable London district of Whitefriars.

Living conditions were deplorable in these primitive shanty towns. A *New York World* correspondent in Washington, Georgia, wrote:

> I have passed places inhabited by crowds of freedmen where in hot summer weather the stench was so great that I had to stop up my nose and cross to the other side of the street.

Finally, the inevitable happened. A smallpox epidemic struck the city late in 1865, and the impoverished, ill-housed blacks became the principal victims. As many as five thousand died, according to one estimate which may have been exaggerated. Former slave Ike Derricotte pointed an accusing finger at his Northern liberators, "Them Yankees brought the smallpox here with them and give it to all the Athens folks, and that was something awful. Folks just died out with it so bad."

Two "mild" cases of smallpox were reported by the *Southern Banner* on September 6, 1865. The paper predicted that "the purity of our climate" would prevent the disease from spreading, but it raged on for about five months.

The town council was forced to erect a special smallpox hospital on the fairgrounds on the old Watkinsville Road in November. The "pest house," as it was called by the freedmen, was small and crudely built. "It warn't near large enough for all de folks dat was sick wid smallpox," commented Derricotte. During its first six weeks of operation, 154 patients were admitted to the facility.

Those who were unable to receive medical treatment at the hospital were forced to resort to home remedies and other more desperate measures. Two black men, Lake Brown and Clarence Bush, were carried off into the swamps and left to die in an effort to prevent further spreading of the disease. "Fore dey got rid of it [smallpox], dey had to burn up beds and clothes and a few houses," according to Paul Smith, a former slave. It was not until February 15, 1866 that the smallpox hospital could close its doors permanently.

During the same five months, blacks who escaped the epidemic were looking forward to their first Christmas after the Jubilee with more than usual anticipation. This was to be the biggest Christmas of all time because the federal government would give each of the,m what they had waited for so long: forty acres and a mule. In fact, they were so sure of getting forty acres and a mule from their former masters that many of the freedmen refused to look for work or take a job that was offered to them.

Obviously disturbed by this attitude among the freedmen, Athenian Howell Cobb wrote to his wife, "I am offering them even better terms than I gave them last year, to whit one-third of the cotton and corn ... but nothing satisfies them ..." In helpless frustration he concluded, "The truth is I am thoroughly disgusted with free negro labor and am determined that the next year shall close my planting operations with them...."

Alexander Stephens testified before the Joint Committee on Reconstruction in Washington in April, 1866 that the belief that property distribution was to occur at Christmas 1865 severely restricted the signing of work contracts for 1866. He maintained that the blacks did not want to bind themselves for the following year because this would probably interfere with the maintenance of their own farms.

In order to squelch the widespread rumor, General Davis Tillson was summoned from Augusta early in December to tell the disappointing truth to the large group of blacks gathered on the university campus: neither the acreage nor the mule would be forthcoming.

Rumors of a black revolt in Athens immediately spread through the white community which became ever more fearful as Christmas approached. The rumors gathered strength as so-called reliable blacks confessed that a rebellion was planned. Besides, white Athenians noticed that freedmen were buying an unusual number of pistols and revolvers.

The white community steeled itself for trouble. Town officials were warned to "keep a sharp lookout" so that whites would not be taken by surprise, and the town council added twenty extra policemen to the regular force of four men. Some blacks near Watkinsville were arrested and jailed in Athens for allegedly helping to plan the rebellion.

The much-discussed insurrection failed to materialize, and Christmas was a quietly festive season in Athens in 1865. It was marred only by the suspicions and prejudices which had been created among both black and white Athenians as they tried to adjust to a new and difficult situation.

Historian Alan Conway suggests that the refusal of the federal government to implement its program of land redistribution bore special political significance to blacks and whites in the South.

> White Georgians realized that the federal government, although a Northern government, was still a white man's government...The more intelligent Negroes also realized this fact. What might have happened had distribution taken place can never be known, but its abandonment served...notice that white men were closing their ranks...

With the arrival of a new year, some of the freedmen put the disappointment of Christmastime behind them and contracted to work for white landowners. The Freedmen's Bureau, which established a post in Athens during the latter months of the previous year, approved all of Col.

David Barrow's contracts with black workers. A short time later one of Barrow's sons reported from their Oglethorpe County plantation that the hands were working "as well as they ever."

Other blacks who had rushed to the city after the Emancipation began to migrate to southwest Georgia and to the fertile Mississippi Valley area. Agents of Mississippi planters came to Athens to recruit local blacks, offering them better wages and the possibility of land ownership. Naturally, Athens whites blamed the Yankees for the exodus of black workers. "The people ... here are having a good deal of trouble about their Negroes, the Yankees are taking them out west," wrote Johnny Cobb, a white resident. Following the departure of a group of freedmen for the Mississippi Valley, the *Southern Watchman* noted in its Negrophobic style: "*The Bouquet D'Afrique* is not quite so strong on our street corners as it was a few days ago."

Although there was some improvement in black-white labor relations in Clarke County, some employers continued to experience difficulties in coping with free black laborers. Mrs. Howell Cobb, Sr., accustomed to complete dominance over her house servants, discovered that emancipated blacks often asserted their own wills. And to her "horror and disgust," the black servants were eating their meals on her finest china.

Another source of white irritation with freed blacks was the constant turnover of servants in the households of Athens' wealthier families. The Cobbs' butler, Robert, departed in search of higher wages, and many letters of that period show that the Cobbs' situation was not unique. In his 1967 study of Reconstruction in Athens, Robert Gamble makes an interesting analysis of this movement among local blacks:

> A closer examination of this flux ... reveals a significant development in the Negro community of the town which lies deeper than mere restlessness, or a search for better wages—an attempt to knit together the fabric of a true family life.

Although there were some exceptions, many blacks desperately sought to locate family members who had been sold away on the auction block at Watkinsville or in various other cities and towns throughout America. "Jack came for Patsy last week and I had to give her up," lamented Olivia Cobb in March 1866. Priscilla Flint Sawyer reported that "Roberta's dear stepfather came for her on New Year's Eve and took her off...."

Tempy, a former slave of Col. David Barrow, left to posterity her request for her two children.

> Mas Davy:
>
> As Christmas is drawing nigh I drop you a few lines in regard to my children, Lizy and Jiles, I spoke to you about sending them to me last Christmas. I am still very anctious for you to send them as I want them with me. 1 can't get my own consent for them to stay away from me longer, please let me hear from you as soon as you can and let me know whether you will send them or not and when you will send them.
>
> Give my regards to all
> Your obedient servant
> Tempy
>
> P.S. If you will send them and advance money to pay their expences I will pay you the money back when Mas Tom settles with me for this years services.
>
> Tempy

There were other tangible signs that the former slaves were slowly beginning to adjust to freedom. A Freedmen's Bureau agent reported that blacks had purchased seventy homes in Athens by the summer of 1867. The first black fire company was organized, and Pierce's Chapel, the city's first black church, held its first meeting in 1866.

During the summer of 1867, blacks and whites paused to celebrate the Fourth of July. With new appreciation for the meaning of freedom and independence, freedmen from all the surrounding counties poured into Athens. It looked like "every Negro in the whole county" had come to Athens to see the "hoisting of the colors and to hear the Yankee brass band play," Evelyn Jackson reported.

All night and into the morning of the holiday she heard wagons filled with freedmen rumbling past her Watkinsville home on the road to Athens. The *Southern Banner* reported, "There was a multitude no man could number, from all points of the compass, and some of them from a distance of fifty or sixty miles… "

Similar celebrations were going on all over the state. Four thousand blacks and whites marched triumphantly through the streets of Augusta. Another ten thousand gathered in Savannah.

But in Athens there was one sour note in the proceedings. A large crowd of blacks flocked to the University of Georgia campus to see the first commencement exercises since the end of the Civil War. When they arrived at the chapel the blacks were stopped, "with some difficulty," at the door. School officials refused to let them witness the ceremony. Ironically, the music at the ceremony was supplied by Billy Holbrooks, Tom Reed, and Wes Brown—three popular local musicians, all of whom were black.

Historian E.M. Coulter's indignation toward this black assault on the previously all-white ivory tower of learning was expressed in his *College Life In The Old South.*

> Instead of respectful slaves grinning and bowing under the campus trees, a swarm of noisy Negroes now determined with the aid of Federal soldiers to put to practical use their newly won freedom, flocked into the chapel. The sheriff drove them out onto the campus where they remained undisturbed. The next year they were warned to stay off the campus entirely....

Of all the things the freedmen needed or desired, land and education were undoubtedly the most important. The federal government quickly defaulted on its promise to supply the former, but with the aid of northern philanthropic organizations, it did establish several hundred freedmen schools throughout the South.

Lerone Bennett writes, "In the first days of freedom—the freedmen demonstrated a passion for education which has never perhaps been equaled in the history of the world." According to eyewitnesses, it appeared as if the entire race wanted to go to school. In January 1867, the first two northern white teachers were sent to Athens by the American Missionary Association, and by the end of the month, almost two hundred blacks were seeking instruction from them. (See Chapter 4.)

For the white citizens of Athens and Clarke County, the defeat of the South and the resultant emancipation of former slaves had been the bitterest of pills to swallow. They too would have to rebuild and start anew under the reign of a new social order. Yet there were those among them who would still long for the way of life that had been buried forever in the pages of history.

> They [slaves] and their like are gone. No more courteous Uncle Miles; no more Aunt Malindas, no bandanna kerchiefs, no hoe cake and fresh butter milks. In their place a spectacled combination of pulpit and the schoolroom. The old place once so full of life is almost deserted. A negro renter is its only tenant—the gin house is gone: the old quarters have rotted down and a mulberry thicket in charity hides the ruins. Master and mistress are dead. The faithful Negroes are but memories of the past.

In general, the white people of Athens were beginning to get used to the idea that slavery had ended. New businesses were opened, religious revivals were held, and the "influx of students of both sexes added life and income to the town."

Early in 1867, Congress passed the first Reconstruction Act which called for the division of the southern states into five military districts, the disenfranchisement of former Confederate officials, and the enfranchisement of the former slaves. The act also required each of the states to ratify the Fourteenth Amendment and to draw up new state constitutions before they would be allowed to rejoin the Union.

The disenfranchisement of former southern officials was particularly alarming to southern whites—including Athenians—who viewed the requirement as the ultimate infringement upon their rights. Although only a few southern whites were actually former Confederate officials, in the minds of many white people the act meant that all blacks would be given the vote and all whites would be disenfranchised.

Blacks, on the other hand, welcomed this legislation and began getting involved in politics. Alfred Richardson, who would one day be one of the first black legislators, began his stormy political career by making what one white Athenian called an "incendiary speech" at one of the political meetings which were becoming a regular occurrence among Athens blacks.

The catalyst for much of the political ferment in the black community was the Union League or Loyal League. Organized in Ohio in 1862, league members pledged themselves to complete loyalty to the federal government. The Union League supported black suffrage and the disenfranchisement of Confederate officials. Its membership was composed of black and white men who were violently opposed to the Ku Klux Klan and the Democratic Party

The Union League made its first appearance in Athens during the summer of 1867 when a black man on horseback, wearing a sash and a sword, led a group of blacks and whites through the streets of the city. The parade ended at an old shop located at the northwest corner of Hull and Hancock streets where the blacks swore to vote the Republican ticket. The old shop became the "site of frequent Union League meetings, members being summoned by the deep blast from a horn" that shattered the early evening quietness of postbellum Athens.

Hundreds of black and white men registered to vote in Clarke County during the summer months as both groups sought to achieve numerical superiority at the polls. The political factions were preparing for the fall elections which would determine if Georgia voters were in favor of calling a constitutional convention so that a new state constitution could be drafted. "The registrar's report in mid-August revealed four hundred and fifty whites as opposed to six hundred seventy-five" black voters registered in the county.

The election was held from October 29 to November 2. The final results revealed there were 684 votes favoring the convention with only one opposed. Although the final voter registration figures showed well over nine hundred white voters in Clarke County, only one of them had voted in the election.

Coulter explains that white Athenians "were deterred by the weird sight of a mass of ignorant and illiterate Negroes, only recently slaves, holding sway at the ballot boxes." But other historians reasoned that the voter boycott was an attempt by white Georgians to take advantage of a provision in the first Reconstruction Act requiring that a majority of the registered voters approve the convention. In any case, the large black voter turnout in Clarke County and other parts of the state resulted in the approval of the constitutional convention.

Convention delegates then met in Atlanta to draft a new state constitution which would have to be approved or disapproved by Georgia voters in April of 1868. A governor, state legislators, and a congressman from the Athens district would also be elected. The first volleys in the political battle between the Radical Republicans and the Conservative Democrats had been fired during the preceding fall. This set the stage for the momentous spring elections in which black candidates would be seeking office for the first time in Clarke County. (See Chapter 2.)

Meanwhile, Athens whites grew angry and frightened as they watched former slaves exercising their new political strength. In some men, hatred and fear erupted into that peculiar brand of terrorism which was the trademark of the Ku Klux Klan.

In Clarke County, groups of twenty or thirty men banded together to form a Klan. They nailed notices of their meetings on the livery stable door using "mysterious words which resisted interpretation by uninitiated persons."Then, dressed in their hoods and sheets, they met and "the word was passed in secret what was to be the night's work."

According to Augustus Hull, this "work" usually consisted of,

> ...visiting the house of some idle negro who had made himself obnoxious, terrifying him with ghostly scenes, whipping him into submission, then warning him that unless there was a radical change in his conduct a second call would prove more disastrous.

Because he was so outspoken, Alfred Richardson, who would become one of the first members of his race to serve in the Georgia legislature, became a favorite target of the Klansmen. After one of their visits, it was reported [erroneously] that he had been killed in a gun battle.

Although initiation of the Southern Reconstruction programs was received with unrestrained optimism by the freedmen, the true condition of Clarke County blacks was one of great disappointment. Racked by disease, ravaged by poverty, and scorned by a majority of their fellow white citizens, the former slaves discovered that the coming of the Jubilee had not brought an end to their many troubles.

They realized they were faced with the monumental task of having to build a free culture and society with the splintered blocks of American slavery. Schools would have to be built, churches would have to be organized, scattered families would have to be reunited.

But regardless of his difficulties and shortcomings, the black man was free—his long-prayed-for Jubilee had finally arrived. Although not totally prepared, the Athens freedmen were willing to accept the privileges and the challenges of American citizenship. In the words of Thomas Johns,

> There is something 'bout being free, and that makes up for all the hardships. I's been both slave and free, and I knows. Course, while I was a slave, I didn't have no 'sponsibility, didn't have to worry 'bout where some

thing to eat and wear and a place to sleep was coming from, but that don't make up for being free.

Madison Davis

TWO LAWMAKERS

From Slave Cabin to State Legislature

Who are your representatives
people of Clarke?
The people have none!
The blacks have elected Mat Davis!?!
and Alfred Richardson!?!

SOUTHERN BANNER

APRIL 24, 1868 ARRIVED IN ATHENS under the cover of low-hanging clouds which produced a steady, annoying drizzle throughout the day. But the rain could not dampen the tenseness that pervaded the city. A sense of history hung in the air.

This day marked the beginning of a four-day voting period in which ballots would be cast for candidates seeking election to both state and national offices. The election was unique because it was the first of its kind to be held in the county since the task of reconstructing the defeated South had been undertaken. It was also the first time that former slaves and slave masters of Clarke County would vote in a contest in which two blacks were seeking election to the Georgia State Legislature from Clarke County.

The rain continued to fall. Some white southerners thought the weather was symbolic of the occasion: "The heavens weep in view of the desecration of this fair land." But the bad weather had little effect on the voter turnout. The line of black and white voters lengthened in front of the Town Hall located on what is now Washington Street. Occupation troops in their blue uniforms kept a wary eye on the ballot box, while they searched the crowd for the first sign of trouble.

But there was none. At least there was no racial conflict. What little trouble there was came from some questionable electioneering tactics near the polls. In fact, the losing candidates later challenged the election results because, they claimed, local freedmen worked too hard to get all black voters to vote for Republican candidates.

According to one Democratic observer, "Smart negroes with a sheaf of tickets in their hands" stood outside the Town Hall to make sure that "every colored voter received the 'right ticket.'" Meanwhile, other blacks were "posted on the steps and all along the way to the window" to make sure the black voters put the right ticket in the right box.

But whites touting the Democratic Party were not idle either. Armed men patrolled the area around Town Hall pretending to keep order, but obviously intending to intimidate voters—especially new black voters—who wanted to vote for the radical Republicans.

Although there was no physical violence around the polls, Alfred Richardson later testified that some whites had intimidated prospective black voters before the election. According to Richardson, several Clarke County blacks told him they were afraid "to vote the way they wanted to" and, unless they could "get protection against the disguised men," they would not vote in future elections.

When the polls finally closed at 6 p.m. on April 28, a racially divided city waited in suspense for the outcome of four days of balloting. The final tabulations revealed that two former slaves, Madison Davis and Alfred Richardson, had been elected to the Georgia General Assembly. The majority of Athens' white citizenry was outraged and a local newspaper expressed the prevailing sentiments:

> We cannot pretend to enumerate a tithe of the villainy openly practiced and attempted here. It is heart sickening and disgusting beyond anything we ever conceived of before.

But the victories of Davis and Richardson were hailed as major achievements by local blacks and whites who sought equality for the former slaves.

Both legislators were present for the called session of the legislature which convened in Atlanta on the Fourth of July, 1868. This particular session of the legislature was unique because twenty-eight black legislators were expelled by their white colleagues. According to one source, "The understanding had been general that the right of the Negro to vote did not give him the right to hold office."

Shortly after the assembly convened, members of the Democratic Party began the campaign that resulted in the ouster of the black members. They directed their initial efforts toward the three black men who had been elected to the Georgia Senate. A. A. Bradley was forced from his seat because he had allegedly been convicted and jailed at one time for seduction in the state of New York. (Seduction was not a felony in Georgia in 1868.) On September 7, a resolution was introduced and subsequently adopted by the senate declaring T. G. Campbell and George Wallace "ineligible to hold office under the Constitution of Georgia and the United States because they were persons of color."

Meanwhile, twenty-five black lawmakers in the Georgia House of Representatives were experiencing the same trouble as the black senators. A resolution declaring the black representatives ineligible had been introduced on August 8, but four days later a counter resolution was made stating "that the question of color should not be entertained in determining the eligibility of its members." This was followed by a report from the Privilege and Election Committee stating once again that the blacks were ineligible.

The committee report further declared that four mulatto legislators, including Madison Davis of Clarke County, were also ineligible to serve in the assembly. But the mulattos were eventually allowed to retain their seats in the house because the leaders of the purge were unable to prove that they were more than "one-eighth Negro."

By mid-August 1868, the entire House of Representatives had become embroiled in a long and bitter debate concerning the eligibility of its black members. The principal defender of the blacks was Henry McNeal Turner, the most famous of the newly elected black lawmakers. On September 3, the last day of the debate, Turner addressed the house in a last-ditch effort to save himself and the other black representatives from expulsion. The legislative chambers fell silent as Turner began his impassioned speech, which lasted four hours.

Mr. Speaker:

Before proceeding to argue this question upon its intrinsic merits, I wish the Members of this House to understand the position that I take. I hold that I am a member of this body—I am here to demand my rights, and to hurl thunderbolts at the men who would dare to cross the threshold of my manhood.

The scene presented in this House, today, is one unparalleled in the history of the world. From this day, back to the day when God breathed the breath of life into Adam, no analogy for it can be found. Never, in the history of the world, has a man been arraigned before a body clothed with legislative, judicial or executive functions, charged with the offense of being of a darker hue than his fellow men.

I stand very much in the position of a criminal before your bar, because I dare to be the exponent of the views of those who sent me here. Or, in other words, we are told that if black men want to speak, they must speak through white trumpets.

Now, sir, I claim to be a citizen, I claim to be an elector, and I claim to be entitled to hold office!

Despite Turner's pleas and the efforts of Georgia Governor Bullock on behalf of the black legislators, the house voted 82-23 in favor of expelling the twenty-five representatives. They were not restored to their seats in the assembly until a congressional mandate reinstated them one-and-a-half years later.

Eleven months after they returned to their rightful places in the legislature, both Richardson and Davis were reelected to second terms. Richardson's stormy career ended during this term when he died quietly of pneumonia at the age of forty after having survived two violent shoot-outs with the Ku Klux Klan.

According to historian Augustus Hull, Richardson was a "turbulent and dangerous Negro" who wreaked "violent measures against the whites." A black man with this kind of reputation was fair game for the Klan. One of Richardson's white neighbors warned him that the Klan was coming, so he was prepared for the twenty-five night riders who raided his Watkinsville home for the second time a month after he was reelected.

The Klansmen forced their way inside and fired at him pointblank. One bullet struck Richardson in his side; the other lodged in his right arm. But he fired back at his attackers as he retreated to the attic, and succeeded in fatally wounding one of them. The Klansmen carried him away as they fled from Richardson's home.

Richardson and his family fled to Athens, where he found a sympathetic reception from white as well as black citizens. Even the generally unsympathetic white press admitted that this was "not the way to punish or intimidate or control the colored people." News of the attack on Richardson spread all the way to Washington. Six months after the attack, a joint committee of Congress investigating the activities of the Ku Klux Klan in the South asked him to testify.

Although all his testimony about the Klan in northeast Georgia was frightening, "Even after a hundred years, one portion of Richardson's narrative leaps hauntingly from the yellowed pages," historian Robert Gamble observed about the following passage.

> A heap of whippings down there have never been reported.... What I am telling you is what people come right to me and tell me. Thousands of things are done down there that are never reported in the papers, and nobody ever knows anything about them.

Alfred Richardson—slave, carpenter, tavern owner, legislator—died in office in 1872. His colleague, Madison "Mat" Davis, introduced resolutions of respect to Richardson's memory in the Georgia General Assembly, which the white members adopted "without much enthusiasm or regret." Davis lived a much longer, more tranquil life by staying away from white troublemakers in Clarke County, and restricting himself to the role of a "sensible" advocate of peace and order, according to Augustus Hull.

His very light skin was both a blessing and a curse to him. Davis was allowed to remain in the legislature because of his "white appearance" during the purge of 1868. But being a mulatto had its drawbacks, too. In Washington, D. C., the white hotel clerk explained, "since you told me that you are colored, you cannot stop at this hotel." Shortly after, the clerk at the black hotel also turned him away claiming, "you are too white for this hotel."

In any case, Davis was an efficient lawmaker with a surprisingly successful record considering the deep feelings of racial animosity that existed in those Reconstruction days. Two of the five bills he introduced into the 1870-71 session were passed. Thanks to one of them, state relief was obtained for Mrs. H. S. Camak, a member of one of Athens' prominent white families, when she fell on hard times in the years following the Civil War.

However, his fellow legislators turned thumbs down on a bill requesting $1,500 for the Athens Fire Department "to enable the Department to protect Franklin University, etc." (Franklin University was the former name of the University of Georgia.) His bill authorizing "the extension of the Georgia Railroad" or the construction of another railway "from Athens to Rabun Gap" was also defeated.

No one knows why Davis abruptly withdrew his name from the ballot in the middle of his third election campaign. We do know he was replaced on the ballot by a black man named Hunter, but the period of black Republican legislative representation in Clarke County was over. Candidate Hunter was soundly defeated and, for the first time since 1868, the county elected two white representatives to the Georgia Legislature.

The *Athens Southern Watchman* joyfully proclaimed: "Old Clarke Redeemed, Regenerated and Disenthralled!" Another local white paper, the *North-East Georgian*, announced in bold letters that "Old Clarke" was herself again: "Negro Representation is a Thing of the Past."

Amid the revelry and celebration, one of the Democratic victors, Dr. Henry Carlton, paused to offer words of consolation to the politically defeated blacks in Clarke County.

> The Doctor begged his friends to treat the colored man with kindness and humanity; he said there never was in the annals of history, a nation so suddenly elevated from slavery to freedom who behaved so well as the blacks had done. ... He thought they would all find that the Southern man was their friend.

"And the Southern man was—as long as the Negro accepted his subordinate posbition," historian Robert Gamble wrote.

But private citizen Davis continued to be a respected, influential leader in the black community as well as Athens at large. After a stint as the United States surveyor of customs in Atlanta, the thirty-three-year-old Davis distinguished himself as captain of Relief No. 2, Clarke County's first black fire company. According to one report,

> When a block of stores on Broad Street burned one fall Saturday night in 1866, the stricken merchants extended their thanks to the colored firemen for their valiant services, "especially Mat Davis and Charles Hill, Captain and Pipeman,.. for their coolness and energy on the occasion."

Finally, at the age of fifty, the man who had been owned by an Athens carriage maker for thirty-two years became the first black man to be appointed postmaster in Athens. Shortly after he assumed this position, Davis became peripherally involved in a bitter congressional campaign between incumbent Emory Speer and Democratic challenger Allen D. Candler.

Although Speer ran as a member of the Independent party, Democrats accused him of collaboration with the Radical Republicans and with black voters. The *Banner-Watchman* threatened to print several letters in its possession that would prove Speer's "compromising correspondence" with black Republicans. The paper insisted that the letters would prove that Speer was personally responsible for the appointment of Mat Davis as postmaster and that Speer was relishing "the degradation he had placed upon his white constituency."

Despite a court order restraining the paper from printing the letters,

> The Athens paper published one letter from Speer to Davis, evading the injunction by the claim that this letter had been picked up on the street and a copy forwarded to the paper by a friend. Addressed to "My dear Mat," the letter gave encouragement regarding the appointment and said, "You are in a position to do me great good with the mountain men...." For the rest of the campaign, Speer was taunted with the "Dear Mat" letter and much was made of his Republican support.

The charges and countercharges became more heated as Election Day approached. Black Clarke County voters, who generally voted in a solid Republican bloc, were sharply divided between Speer and Candler. When a Republican mass rally was held at the Athens Town Hall on October 2, 1882, the meeting turned into a Speer rally headed by Davis, and many Candler supporters left in disgust.

Angered by Davis's endorsement of Speer, the Candler supporters removed him from the chairmanship of the Clarke County Republican Executive Committee. Other blacks refused to vote for Speer because he was not a registered Republican. The former black legislator angrily denounced them as "Republican renegades" and "traitors to race and party." Despite his efforts, Speer was defeated, and the Republican Party suffered yet another defeat in northeast Georgia.

Davis died after a lifetime of moral, political, and community leadership, and was buried in the Gospel Pilgrim Cemetery near Springfield Baptist Church on Fourth Street.

Although many Georgia historians have tended either to ignore them or brand them ignorant, corrupt and ineffective, a survey of legislative records and journals during the Reconstruction period suggests that the black legislators may have deserved a more favorable treatment by state historians.

In spite of the prejudices, even violence, which marred their political careers, Davis and Richardson left their mark on the political and social climate of Georgia, and contributed to the overall strength of the Republican Party. They and the other black lawmakers who served in the Georgia Legislature between 1868 and 1871 helped to implement many reforms and improvements that paved the way for Georgia's future development.

The public schools in Georgia, elementary through college; the elimination of barbarous forms of punishment, such as the whipping post and the flogging of naked female prisoners; the enfranchisement of women; the establishment of equal accommodations on public conveyances; and the enfranchisement of thousands of white males who had been denied the right to vote because they lacked material wealth—these are just a few of the reforms that can be traced back to Georgia's black Reconstruction legislators.

"These Negroes deserve a place in the history of Georgia," historian Ethel Maude Christler wrote in 1932, "not because they were the first Negroes to take an active part in her politics, but because of the constructive work accomplished by them." In addition, Davis, Richardson, and the other blacks proved by example that former slaves could be entrusted with the responsibility for writing the laws of their state, and for representing all the people in their districts.

EDITOR'S NOTE: Davis and Richardson were the last African Americans to be elected to the Georgia legislature by Clarke County voters for more than 100 years. In 1986, after two defeats, Michael Thurmond, an Athens lawyer, won election to the House of Representatives of the Georgia General Assembly. Keith Heard, an African-American Athenian, succeeded Thurmond in the legislature in 1992.

Representative Keith Heard

THE BLACK CHURCH

Not by Faith Alone

There is a religion that takes off fetters
instead of binding them on,
that breaks every yoke,
that lifts up the bowed down....

FREDERICK DOUGLASS

First A.M.E. Choir in the 1930s

It is the second sunday in August. The church is packed with a perspiring, expectant brood of black humanity. Wasps buzz undisturbed through raised windows. Big-breasted women fan against the hot and motionless air. The sorrowful moan that originates in the deacons' corner transforms itself into a familiar hymn, complete with the rhythmic thump of feet on the wooden floor. Song and sounds mingle to form a spiritual catalyst which excites those trapped by the music's hypnotic grip.

Without warning, the hymn ends amid a chorus of *amens* and *praise the Lords*. Before the gathered multitude a commanding black figure assumes the center stage. He reads the selected text, pauses, and the preaching begins. Effortless words pour from his mouth in constantly louder, more emphatic tones.

His body, anchored by a crippled leg, gyrates and twists in perfect punctuation to his spoken words. Sweat beads appear on the preacher's forehead as he plunges deeper into his sermon on hell fire and brimstone. Preacher, sermon, choir and congregation slowly merge into rhythmic litany.

The preacher screams, "One day we all gon' have to meet our Maker!"

"That's right!" the worshipers respond.

"One daaay—we all gon' have to account for our sins!"

"Preach it, brother!" comes the response.

True to form, the elder deacon's hoarse, ancient voice is heard over the commotion: "Take your time brother, take your time. "

The Spirit descends upon the congregation. Predictably, the now childless mother is the first to succumb to the invisible power. She shivers uncontrollably and leaps to her feet, questioning and yet accepting the wisdom of His will. The raging spiritual contagion spreads with frightening rapidity, as white-clad ushers rush to restore order throughout the now frenzied congregation.

The worshipers are swept back—back to an ancient, mysterious land of primitive rituals and ecstatic ceremonies. Their spirits have been transported to an ancient place and time that no longer exists. And so it is that the unique phenomenon of the black church in America has survived. Significantly changed but basically unaltered from its original form—a form that is firmly rooted in both African and American soil.

This assimilation of divergent religious backgrounds began in Athens, as in most sections of this nation, during the years of slavery. Before and during the Civil War, "four of Athens' white churches—the Baptist, Methodist, Presbyterian, and Episcopal— all had Negro members." As early as 1826, Dr. Lovick Pierce, pastor of the First Methodist Church, reported to his annual conference: "Membership, whites 107, colored 70, and a total collection of $9.41 from Athens and Madison."

Between 1844 and 1845, a "wondrous revival" was held during which 97 Negroes and 163 whites were converted to the Methodist faith.

> Following this revival, the colored membership had become so large that they demanded a church and pastor of their own, and the annual conference sent Rev. John M. Bonnell, a white man, as their pastor.

The Methodists and the Baptists each maintained a chapel for their black worshipers, while the Presbyterian and Episcopal churches set aside the galleries for Negro members.

The most significant revival of the antebellum period in Athens began in the white Methodist church in March 1858, spreading to the white Baptist church in early April, and from there to other local congregations. Large numbers of black and white Athenians were converted during the protracted revival, with the black Methodist church registering an increase of more than one hundred members. Meetings continued until early May in the white churches and for several weeks after that in the black Methodist church.

It is important to note that one of the principal motives behind the slave master's desire to Christianize his black bondsmen was not so much that their "heathen souls might be saved," as it was to ensure the continued existence of the slave-master relationship. Many slave owners were quick to realize the importance of religious doctrine which, if taught in the correct manner, would place a moral and spiritual block between the slave and his desire for freedom. One unidentified slave recalls the nature and ultimate purpose of so-called slave Christianity:

> The Blacks sat in the back of the church as the white minister preached and directed the following text at them: Don't steal your master's chickens or his eggs and your backs won't be whipped.

The slaves reacted to their masters' religion by holding "secret services, bush arbor meetings or prayer meetings in the swamps." The same master who required attendance at Sunday sermons often punished with the lash those he caught at these secret meetings.

Many of the rural churches in Clarke and surrounding counties predate the end of the Civil War. These religious institutions often began as secret churches whose meetings were held under trees or in bush groves. It is interesting to note that several of the rural black churches still in existence have names that probably indicate the nature of their origins—Shady Grove, Chestnut Grove, and Billups Grove, for example.

One obvious indication of the black man's dissatisfaction with slave religion was the speed with which he moved to organize his own churches following the Emancipation. The first church organized by blacks in Athens was Pierce's Chapel African Methodist Episcopal (A.M.E.) Church, which held its first meeting in 1866 in a building "under the hill" between downtown and the Oconee River. It was named for The Rev. Lovick Pierce, mentioned above, who helped church members locate a building to worship in.

By March of the following year, Pierce's Chapel had 254 members. Later the congregation changed its name to First A.M.E, and in 1916 they built the present building on Hull Street.

Hill First Baptist Church is the oldest black Baptist church in Athens. It was organized approximately one year after Pierce's Chapel in April of 1867. A history of the church states that the Rev. Floyd Hill, in response to a vision, withdrew his congregation from the white congregation and began to build the present church. The separation of blacks from whites in the local Baptist church was apparently done without hostility, as evidenced by the fact that the white Baptists "permitted the Negroes continued use of the . . . chapel" in the white church even after the black church was founded.

During the last quarter of the nineteenth century, several new black churches were organized in and around Athens. They were founded when dissident factions separated from an established church, or when members of a new denomination appeared on the scene.

Included among the dissidents would be Hill Chapel Baptist Church which was organized in 1892 because of differences between members of Hill First Baptist. Among the latter group of newcomers were the Congregationalists (American Missionary Association—A.M.A.), who held their first meeting in 1881. Their church was closely associated with the A.M.A.-supported Knox Institute.

> Unable to afford a building, the congregation met in the basement of Knox for ten years. Finally in 1890, donations from the A.M.A. and from Congregationalists all over the East enabled the Athens congregation to build their own church.

The organization of Landrum Baptist Church came as a direct result of the efforts of the Reverend Collins H. Lyons, a black Baptist minister. Before the Civil War, Landrum Chapel had been occupied by a predominantly white congregation. In 1878, Lyons and thirteen other original members met for the first time in the abandoned Landrum Chapel on the southeast corner of Mitchell and Thomas streets. They met there for several years, eventually renaming the church Ebenezer Baptist and relocating in a new building on the west side of Athens.

Negro Church Used as School

The ability of the early black churches to raise funds from their congregations was one of the principal reasons for their relative financial stability. The so-called table method of collection was and still is used in some churches. It permits the giver to walk to the front of the church, in full view of the congregation, to deposit his or her contribution on the collector's table. (T.J. Woofter, a white historian, cynically observed that this method was successful because it took advantage of the black man's "love of display.")

It was common practice during the earlier stages of their development for local black churches to turn out church members who were accused or convicted of various wrongdoings. A typical incident occurred in 1895 when the Congregationalist Church excommunicated eleven persons even though it needed members. Sometimes punitive measures were taken even against people at the top of the church hierarchy. The Reverend J.W. Gardener, pastor of Hill First Baptist Church, was forced to resign in 1896 after he was "accused of being a Methodist and various other shortcomings."

In the late 1870s, a large number of people were converted to the Christian faith during a very successful religious revival in the black community. This set the stage for one of the largest baptisms ever recorded in the city of Athens. The event, which was held in the Oconee River just below the Oconee Street Bridge, drew the attention of hundreds of people who gathered on the banks of the river to watch the ceremony.

Although the baptism was intended to be conducted in a solemn, religious manner, an unlikely turn of events introduced the threat of tragedy combined with comedy which dissolved the pious atmosphere. Wooden stakes were used to mark the shallow waters in order to protect the participants from the deeper, potentially dangerous areas, and everything proceeded according to plan at first. Then suddenly things got out of hand.

> One of the converts was a huge woman who began to shout that she "was crossin' the River Jordan" and the preacher had his hands full in his efforts to quiet her. This seemed to increase her ecstasy; she grabbed him and shoved him into deep water... The preacher was in trouble, for he could not swim, and the crowd was tremendously excited as he floundered and sputtered in deep water.

Believing that the sound of a religious hymn might be of some spiritual or emotional aid to the minister, someone in the crowd called, "Sing something! Sing something," to the director of the choir. He responded by leading the choir in singing "Pull for the shore, sailor, pull for the shore"—a song which happened to be one of the popular Sunday School hymns of that period.

But the singing proved to be of little help to the minister in his life-and-death struggle with the muddy waters of the Oconee. Friends who were watching the episode from the river banks finally rushed into the water and pulled the exhausted preacher to safety. After a few moments' rest, the determined little minister dutifully completed the baptism of the zealous woman.

By 1912, there were twelve black churches in Athens distributed among the several denominations. Five were Baptist and four Methodist; one was Congregational, one Episcopal, and one Sanctified. All of these churches had wood-frame buildings except the First Baptist Church which held its services in a brick edifice. The church buildings averaged about $3,000 in value, and were reported to be free of debt in 1913. Their ministers were paid from twenty-five to forty dollars a month. According to Peter Schinkel,

> The churches became the most important institutions in the Negro community in Athens and even more so in rural Clarke County. They provided the blacks with religious and moral guidance and with the hope of a better life in the hereafter...

In 1915, there were seventeen black churches in Clarke County: fourteen Baptist, two Methodist, and one Primitive Baptist. Eleven of the fourteen black Baptist churches were in the Jeruel Association which supported Jeruel Academy (Union Baptist Institute) in Athens. The other three were members of the Northwestern Association which contributed money to a Negro industrial school in Monroe, Georgia.

The following table, compiled in 1915 by a Phelps-Stokes Fund researcher, summarizes the characteristics of Clarke County's black Baptist churches during that period:

Name of Church	District	Property	Age, Yrs.	Membership	Salary	How often Preaching*	Church Societies	Sunday School Membership
Central	B.B.	1,000	22	200	$25	1	1	35
Shiloh	B.B.	800	30	30	175	1		60
Morton's Chapel	Pur.	1,020	15	400	180	1	1	100
Bethel	S.C.	600	20	50	75	1(3)		30
New Grove	B.B.	1,500	20	237	185	1(2)		75
New Shiloh	S.C.	700	10	65	140	1	1	35
St. James	Kin.	575	1/2	180	125	1(2)	1	40
Thankful	Prin.	300	20	52	75	2		30
Mt. Pleasant	Ath.	800	2	160		2		30
Billups Grove	B.B.	400	1	15	150	1(2)	1	55
Timothy	Prin.	100	15	104	150	1	1	25
Chestnut Grove	Prin.	1,000	8	163	125	1(2}	1	25
St. Mary's	S.C.	1,500	15	150	125	1(3)		35
Mt. Sinai		------	--	----	----	----	---	-----

*The first figure indicates the number of Sundays in the month on which services were held. The figure in parenthesis shows the total number of services held.

None of the seventeen black rural churches employed a fulltime pastor. Five shared their pastor with another congregation; six had pastors serving two other churches; and six others had pastors who preached at three other churches. In addition to regular preachers, the black churches used the services of volunteer or lay preachers. Like their city counterparts, black worshipers in Clarke County displayed a "disposition to favor the preacher who [could] put on the 'rousements' and get the congregation to a high pitch of emotion."

In fact, the Holy Rollers flourished in Athens during the first and second decades of the twentieth century. Their brand of worship was marked by long frenzied church meetings and so-called holy dancing. This denomination, which is now defunct, apparently experienced a great deal of popularity among local blacks. Its membership swelled when members of the Methodist and Baptist churches deserted their former denominations in order to join the more religiously expressive churches.

Rural churches were not only the center of religious activities, but the hub of educational and social activities as well. Church buildings were often used as schoolhouses during the week, and for large social gatherings. (See Chapter 4.) In addition:

> The high point of the rural church year was a two or three day revival held at the end of the summer. Blacks came to the revival from far and near, bringing food and drink and making the revival the social event of the year.

As their memberships increased, the black churches of Athens and Clarke County gained a great deal of power and influence in the black community. Sometimes this influence transcended local boundaries when local religious leaders were elected to church positions of state and national prominence.

At least five churchmen, who were either born or lived in Athens at one time, became bishops of their respective denominations: Lucius Holsey, a former Athens slave; W.H. Heard, co-founder of Athens' first black newspaper; W.D. Johnson, cofounder of *Progressive Era*; J.A. Bray and A.J. Carey, both local educators.

Although she was not a member of the clergy, Julliette Derricotte devoted her life to religious activities. Born in Athens in 1897, her influence extended far beyond her native city. Her work as a Young Women's Christian Association organizer eventually elevated her to membership in the General Commission of the World Christian Federation. Following her election to the commission, Derricotte was sent on a worldwide speaking tour on behalf of the religious organization.

The vast network of lodges that flourished in the black community immediately before and after the turn of the century was apparently an outgrowth of the churches in Athens and Clarke County. The lodges combined "a secret ritualistic feature with a mutual insurance company." Each lodge sponsored elaborate social events, gave deceased members pompous funerals, and dressed in distinctive uniforms on special occasions.

Negro Church, School and Lodge Hall in Puryear's Militia District

The insurance plans sponsored by the lodges were the principal recruiting tools of these secret organizations. When one of the lodge members became ill or died, the lodge would extend financial assistance to his or her family. The lodges usually maintained a sick committee whose members visited and cared for those who were bedridden.

There were twenty-nine lodges representing eight orders in Clarke County in 1912: Good Samaritans, Odd Fellows, Masons, Knights of Pythias, Gospel Pilgrims, Ancient Knights, Independent Benevolent Order, and Magnolias. All but the last two orders had more than one lodge in the city. The Good Samaritans led the list with seven lodges. Estimated membership of the twenty-nine lodges was twenty-five hundred people, or about *75 percent* of the adult black population of Athens in 1912!

The lodges continued as important social and financial institutions throughout the 1920s, until monetary hardships produced by the depression forced many members to forego their financial obligations to the lodges. In addition, some of them suffered damaged reputations when leadership positions fell into the hands of unscrupulous individuals who diverted funds for their own use from organizational treasuries.

In his early twentieth-century study of the black community in Athens, Woofter noted that black churchgoers expressed their religious emotions in various ways, but the "most common outlet" was in songs of "a weird metre which are only heard in Negro churches." The genesis and importance of the spirituals Woofter was referring to is summarized this way by one authority:

> Little of beauty has America given the world save the rude grandeur God himself stamped on her bosom; the human spirit in this new world has expressed itself in vigor and ingenuity rather than in beauty. And so by fateful chance the Negro folksong—the rhythmic cry of the slave—stands today not simply as the sole American music, but as the most beautiful expression of human experience born this side of the seas. It has been neglected, it has been, and is, half despised—but notwithstanding, it still remains as the singular spiritual heritage of the nation and the greatest gift of the Negro people.

It was through the coded messages of the spirituals that the slave spoke to the world and expressed his innermost emotions. The origins of many of these songs have been erased by the passage of time. Some are transmutations of hymns heard by slaves in the churches of their white masters. But others, like "Nobody Knows de Trouble I See," one of the most sorrowful of the sorrow songs, had a more dramatic beginning.

Shortly after the end of the Civil War, the federal government realized it could not fulfill its promise to give forty acres and a mule to the former slaves. A brigadier general was therefore ordered to carry the disappointing news to a large group of blacks living on the Sea Islands off the Georgia-Carolina coast.

After he made his unwelcome announcement, an old black woman standing near the edge of the group began singing the song. The other blacks picked up the chant—singing and swaying to the mournful tempo. It is said that the general stood and wept.

Still other songs speak of the black slave's desire to "go home"— to "cross over the River Jordan" to freedom or to a better life in the hereafter. The field hand's desire to end his seemingly endless toil can be heard and felt in the following lines:

> Dere's no rain to wet you,
> Dere's no sun to burn you,
> Oh, push along, believer,
> I want to go home.

But W.E.B. Dubois makes this interesting observation:

> Through all the sorrow of the Sorrow Songs there breathes a hope—a faith in the ultimate justice of things. The minor cadences of despair change often to triumph and calm confidence. Sometimes it is faith in life, sometimes a faith in death, sometimes assurance of boundless justice in some fair world beyond. But which ever it is, the meaning is always clear: that sometime, somewhere, men will judge men by their souls and not by their skins.

In any case, spirituals like the ones Woofter heard in Athens churches are perhaps the most unique contribution of the black man to American culture. They remain an integral part of the black religious experience. Born and nurtured during the days of slavery, these "sorrow songs" have been regarded by most musicians as "the purest and most valuable musical ore in America; the raw materials of a native American music."

Indeed, the faith embodied in these spirituals served as the foundation of the black church in Athens and in America. Through this faith, the black church and its leaders have organized to challenge the forces of evil and injustice. And with this faith, the struggle will continue.

THE KNOX HERALD.

Vol. 12. ATHENS, GA., May, 1914. No. 3.

Knox Institutute & Industrial School: Under the Auspices ot the A. M. A.—Carnegie Hall.

KNOX INSTITUTE

Athens, Georgia

Under the supervision of the American Missionary Association, Congregational Rooms, Fourth Avenue and Twenty Second Street, New York City.

SECRETARIES:

Rev. H. Paul Douglass, D. D.,
Rev. C. J. Ryder, D. D.,
Honorary Secretary and Editor:
Rev. A. F. Beard, D. D.,

TREASURER:

Mr. Irving C. Gaylord.

Enrollment

1913—1914 377

For catalogue and information write to L. S. Clark, Principal, Knox Institute and Industrial School, Athens, Ga.

Opening Day

KNOX INSTITUTE & INDUSTRIAL SCHOOL Athens, Ga., begins its work, **Wednesday, September** 16th, 1914. The **dormitories** will be opened for the reception of students, **Tuesday, September** 15, 1914. It is hoped that all students will enter promptly on the FIRST DAY. All are welcome.

Courses.—Standard College Preparatory, Grammar, Intermediate, Primary, Domestic Science and Art, Teachers' Training Course, Commercial Course, Industrial, Musical, Kindergarten.

Industrial Work.—Carpentry, mechanical drawing, knife work, sewing, dressmaking, millinery, cooking, typesetting, printing.

Buildings and Equipment.—The **Best Equipped** institution in northeast Georgia in all the departments of literary and industrial work for colored youths. Our 4 buildings are heated by steam, lighted by electricity, and modern in all their equipment.

Board and Tuition.—Our dormitories are in charge of an experienced matron and an experienced preceptress. Board and tuition may be obtained at reasonable rates. Write the Principal for rates.

continued on next page.

EDUCATORS & THEIR SCHOOLS

Quenching the Thirst for Knowledge

Boy, you got to git an education
cause dat's gon' be the only way out for ya.
Son, you git dat education,
cause what's in your head
can't no man take away.

GRANDMA BARCIE BURTON

Despite the dialect, the message has always been clear. The personal drama of illiterate blacks urging their youth to acquire the education they did not possess has been repeated on countless occasions.

Although it was once a crime to teach enslaved blacks how to read and write, cloaked in secrecy, the teaching continued. Finally, when slavery was abolished, the effort to quench the black man's thirst for knowledge was begun with the help of sympathetic whites.

In most Southern states during the Reconstruction period, one of the first tasks undertaken by the Freedmen's Bureau, the federal agency in charge of implementing the Southern Reconstruction programs was the establishment of schools for former slaves. Athens blacks made it known in no uncertain terms that they not only *wanted* educational training but were willing, on at least two occasions, to fight for the privilege. Shortly after emancipation, a group of blacks assembled near the University of Georgia campus and prepared to seize control of the recently reopened institution.

E.M. Coulter wrote, "the motley group of dusky educational warriors ... began to jeer their more fortunate white brothers." Town marshals arrived on the scene and unsuccessfully attempted to disperse the freedmen. University students finally succeeded in routing the blacks by unleashing a volley of gunfire in the general direction of the group.

Late in 1867, "the thirst for higher education gained the ascendance again" among a group of blacks who, after arming themselves with "sticks, clubs and every kind of weapon obtainable," made a second attempt to seize control of Georgia's principal citadel of higher learning. "The students, some armed with guns they had carried through the Civil War, gathered to defend their alma mater..." A heated battle was averted by the intervention of a Professor Mell who convinced the freedmen to leave the campus.

In response to the strong educational demands of local blacks, Freedmen's Bureau agents established the Knox School in Athens in the spring of 1868. A report by the bureau stated that excellent school buildings for blacks were erected in Athens and in five other Georgia cities.

Students at the freedmen schools were usually taught by northern white women who felt a religious calling to instruct the former slaves in the rudiments of reading, writing, and arithmetic. The first four Yankee schoolmarms to teach at the Knox School were Miss E.C. Ayer, Miss M.E. Dyer, Miss E.F. Fitch, and Miss Sara Vannest.

These "nigger teachers," as they were called by some southern whites, met stiff resistance from those who believed that educated blacks were dangerous and untrustworthy. Although actual physical violence against the teachers was rare, the more destructive method of social ostracism made life very difficult for them.

A teacher stationed in Greensboro, Georgia in 1868 described the trouble that he and his fellow teachers encountered when they attempted to secure housing in that city:

> We applied at six places, three of which were boarding houses but none of them would board a "nigger" teacher—I have good reason to believe that there is an understanding between the people of Greensboro to keep out Yankee "nigger" teachers.

A group of white Athenians vented their resentment of the education of blacks by disrupting classes at the Knox School and forcing the white teachers to leave the building in November of 1868. The local press described the Athens teachers as "pious young females of the Puritan persuasion" who, according to one historian, performed a disservice when they dangled "before the Negroes the educational Utopia and innocently awakened in the African heart longings for what could not be."

But there were others who possessed somewhat different opinions of the teachers and their educational work in the Reconstruction South. General Oliver O. Howard, head of the Freedmen's Bureau, called them "the rank and file in the long fight with prejudice and ignorance." M. Hippeau, a French educational researcher wrote, "It would be impossible to convey an idea of the energy and friendly rivalry displayed by the women of America in this truly Christian work..."

Since it was already an educational center, it is not surprising that Athens became the focal point of black undergraduate education in Georgia during the fifty years after the end of the Civil War. The quality and prestige of these schools for black students were equaled by very few black institutions in the South.

KNOX INSTITUTE

Knox School, the first school for blacks in Athens, opened in 1868. It was named in honor of Major John J. Knox, a white Freedmen's Bureau agent, who had been assigned the duty of directing the Reconstruction programs in Athens. (The school was later renamed Knox Institute and Industrial School.)

By 1901, Knox Institute was advertising itself in the *Athens Clipper*, a local black newspaper, as having a "Literary Depart-ment unsurpassed by that of any institution for colored youths in northeast Georgia." The school also had a highly developed industrial department that offered courses in carpentry, type-setting, printing, and sewing.

In 1913, Knox Institute expanded its curriculum to cover twelve grades, and in 1921 earned the distinction of being the "first high school for Negroes ever accredited by the Accrediting Commission of the University of Georgia." In addition to regular grades, there was a special department of music and domestic science.

Carpentry class at Knox Institute

Class in typesetting and printing, Knox Institute

The school grew steadily, and eventually became the largest and one of the most prestigious private schools in Athens. During the 1924-25 school year, a total of 339 students were enrolled, representing five states, twenty-eight counties, and thirty-eight cities and towns.

Located at the corner of Pope and Reese streets, the Knox campus consisted of a girls' dormitory, boys' dormitory, principal's office, and Carnegie Hall. Money for the latter building was donated by philanthropist Andrew Carnegie in 1912. The three-story brick structure was "steam-heated, electric-lighted, contained all modern conveniences, and [was] modern in all its equipment." It contained twenty-one rooms. The first floor was used by the industrial department, and the second and third floors were set aside for literary work.

One of the influential figures in the development of Knox Institute was the Rev. Lewis S. Clarke. He became principal of the institution around 1886, and remained in that position until Knox closed its doors in 1928. Clark's wife also served as a teacher, matron, and preceptress at the school for approximately thirty years. During their tenures, Knox grew from a small "ungraded school with few students to be one of the top-ranking schools for Negroes."

The teachers of Knox Institute were, for the most part, trained at Atlanta and Fisk universities. In 1912, they were paid about $35 per month—$25 in money, plus $10 worth of board and lodging in the school.

Originally supported by the Freedmen's Bureau, Knox later came under the auspices of the American Missionary Association. Other revenues were received from philanthropic organizations and by the collection of tuition and fees from students. In 1912, tuition ranged from 50¢ per month in the primary grades to $1.50 per month in instrumental music courses.

Knox Institute operated for approximately sixty years. When financial difficulties in the late 1920s caused the American Missionary Association to cut off funding to the institution, it was forced to close its doors. In 1933, the city of Athens leased its main building, Carnegie Hall, to house Athens High and Industrial School. During the years the public school was located there, the campus grew to eight structures, including a gymnasium built with funds raised in a campaign led by longtime PTA president Bertha Eberhardt. A.H.I.S. remained in this location until the new school opened on Dearing Extension in 1956.

HEARD UNIVERSITY

J. Thomas Heard University was the smallest of the four black private schools operating in Athens in 1912. It had only a six-year curriculum, but J. Thomas Heard, the black lawyer who founded the school, named it a university so that, in the words of his wife, "it may some day grow into a university, and be a factor in the uplift of his race."

Heard's wife helped to operate the school and teach its seventy-eight students. She taught during the day, and shared evening teaching duties with her husband. (Heard University gave working students the opportunity to attend classes in the evenings in addition to the regular day classes.)

The school was located adjacent to Knox Institute, and this, according to T.J. Woofter, created a major problem.

> It would have been more fortunate had this school been located in some other part of town. It is on the lot next to Knox Institute and, consequently, there is no good will lost between the schools.

THE METHODIST SCHOOL

Little is known about the history of this institution. It was probably founded in 1876 by William H. Heard, co-founder of the *Athens Blade*, Athens' first black newspaper. The school was located on Hancock Avenue in the basement of the Negro Methodist Church. Carrie Pledger was listed in the 1889 Athens Directory as the principal of the institution. Although the exact date of its demise is not known, the Methodist School had ceased operations by 1912.

JERUEL ACADEMY/UNION BAPTIST INSTITUTE

Conflicting accounts exist concerning the identity of the founder(s) of the Jeruel Normal School. Two sources credit the Rev. Collins Lyons with being the founder of the institution. Another source states that the Revs. E.D. Jennings, A.R. Davenport, H.M. Smith, Jesse R. Callaway, and J.Y. Fambro were the principal founders.

But all sources agree that Jeruel opened its doors for the first time in 1881, and was originally supported by a group of mostly rural black churches known as the Jeruel Baptist Association. The first classes were held in Landrum Baptist Church, which stood at the corner of Mitchell and Thomas Streets. After "two or more years of precarious existence," the school's name was changed to Jeruel Academy, "a name more suited to the kind of work sought to be accomplished."

In 1886, Jeruel moved its facilities to the corner of Pope and Baxter streets, where it remained until its closure in 1956. During the years between 1886 and 1956, the school experienced three more name changes. Sometime before 1914, the school changed its name to Jeruel Baptist Institute, and in 1924 it was renamed Union Baptist Institute. The latter name change was the result of the consolidation of the educational efforts of the Union Middle River, the Northwestern No. 1, the Madison, and the Jeruel Baptist associations.

Jeruel faculty in 1901, Principal J.H. Bown, front row, left

JERUEL BAPTIST INSTITUTE, ATHENS, GEORGIA
Under Auspices of Jeruel Baptist Association

The Pioneer Institution for Negro Education in North East Georgia.

Offers the best inducement for the training of negro youths. Located on high elevation; healthful surroundings, in a good community. Training thorough. A competent Faculty from both Southern and Northern Colleges.

A home for Boys and Girls. Utmost care in Management. Work provided for a limited number of students.

The institute offers superior facilities and advantages. A center from which radiates an influence that will affect for good, the home and community life of the student. The farmer is reached through the Annual Farmers' Conference Course of Instruction. The Academy, which prepares for College Entrance, Elementary English, leading to the Academy. Primary, kindergarten. Three Years' Course in Theology, Music Department most Thorough in North East Georgia. Industries: Sewing, plain and artistic, Cooking. Regulations are such as characterize a well governed home. School management parental. Charges are reasonable. Correspondence solicited. School opens September, 1914.

—From *Daily Herald,* special edition, 1914

During the mid-1950s, the Union board of trustees voted to delete the word *Baptist* from the school's name. The trustees made this change because the school had "out grown the narrow path in serving humanity" and was opening its doors "to all denominations and creeds without let or hindrance and on even basis."

The Baptist institution was the second largest private black school in Athens in 1912, with a student enrollment of 197. Jeruel was equipped with boarding residences, which facilitated attendance by students from surrounding counties.

By 1914, the Baptist school had amassed a "competent faculty from both Southern and Northern Colleges," and was offering its students "superior facilities and advantages." The curriculum included college preparatory courses, elementary English, kindergarten, theology, and a "Music Department [the] most thorough in northeast Georgia." Industrial courses, which included sewing—plain and artistic—and cooking, were also offered.

Union Baptist had a physical plant that consisted of a chapel, classrooms, library, laboratories, a twenty-room girls' dormitory, and an eight-room residence with bedrooms for boys.

One of the early principals of the school was Professor J.H. Brown who served as the principal of the institution for approximately thirty-six years, beginning in October of 1886. He advocated racial cooperation and believed blacks needed the help of white people in order to carry out their educational projects.

Whenever possible, he would call on white speakers to address his meetings. Each year, Professor Brown held a Farmer's Conference at his school. The two-fold purpose of the conference was "first, to help the farmers by giving them better methods; and second, to arouse the interest of surrounding rural sections in the work of his school."

The conference often drew the attention of agriculturalists of local and national prominence, including such well-known personalities as Chancellor David C. Barrow of the University of Georgia; Dr. George

Washington Carver, Tuskegee Institute; and Professor J. Phil Campbell of the Agricultural College. According to a 1914 newspaper article, the school had "the fullest cooperation of these gentlemen" in the planning and staging of the annual affair.

Jeruel Academy/Union Baptist Institute

One of Union's most outstanding alumni was Professor C.H. Lyons, Sr., who devoted his life to the uplift of his people. Lyons graduated from Jeruel Academy in 1901. After receiving an advanced degree from Atlanta Baptist College, he returned to his alma mater as an instructor in 1908. Fourteen years later he was appointed the general manager (principal) of Union Baptist Institute.

Lyons held the top position at Union until the school was incorporated into the public school system. During his tenure, the school increased its enrollment and improved the quality of its educational services. Following his death in 1955, Lyons Junior High School was named in his honor, making him the first black man ever to be recognized in this way by the Clarke County School District.

Both Union Baptist and Knox participated in men's and women's interscholastic and intercollegiate athletics. The two Athens schools played athletic schedules that included many black schools in the Southeast, including Paine, Morehouse, and Atlanta University. Naturally, bitter athletic rivalry developed between the two church-supported institutions. The Knox-Union athletic grudge matches were sometimes accompanied by name calling and fistfights between the schools' supporters.

Following an embarrassing defeat by the Knox football team in 1922, Professor Charles Lyons began looking for a new football coach for Union Baptist. He eventually hired a twenty-one-year-old World War I veteran named Harry "Squab" Jones.

Born in 1902, Jones quit school and enlisted in the army at the age of fifteen. After serving in France, he returned to Athens and began a coaching, managing, and training career that would span over half a century. During that period, he served on every level of athletic competition—high school, collegiate, semi-professional, and professional—including being a trainer for many years for the University of Georgia football team. He died in 1990 at the age of 87.

Jones made his coaching debut in the fall of 1923 against Union's arch-rivals from Knox Institute. Although Jones' memory of the game is faded and colored with nostalgia, he recalls that it was a tightly contested, hard-hitting affair. The game developed into a scoreless defensive struggle with neither team possessing the ability to mount a successful offensive drive.

Of course, such an epic contest was deserving of nothing less than a storybook ending. According to Jones, he called on a fleet reserve halfback by the name of Eddie "Ape" Pauldoe in the waning stages of the contest. With the coach's special instructions firmly planted in his mind, Pauldoe grabbed the pigskin on the ensuing play and streaked across the goal line with the game-winning touchdown. Jones testifies that it was a disheartened and thoroughly beaten Knox football team that walked off the playing field on that fall afternoon.

Knox Institute's football team and coach

Second only to the fierce rivalry that existed between Knox and Union was the mutual animosity the two schools shared for the Yellow Jackets of Athens High and Industrial School. Coach Jones still laments the fact that he "never could beat that crowd from Athens High and Industrial." The closest Jones and his Union football team ever came to defeating the squad was in 1924. He is certain that if the referee had not been the opposing coach's brother-in-law, Union would have defeated their public school opponents that year.

Union Baptist Institute remained open longer than any of the black private schools in Athens. It eventually became part of the public school system and served as the high school for students living in Clarke County. The consolidation of city and county school systems forced "the Baptist School on the Hill" to close its doors after seventy-five years of service. There is an historical marker at Brumby Hall on the UGA campus, commemorating its site.

HYMAN LIANA SCHOOL AND HOME

Founded by Miss N.N. Hyman in 1915, the school enrolled about thirty students who came from very poor black families in Athens. Hyman Liana was located in a small building donated by the local white Presbyterian Church.

ROSA SMITH NORMAL SCHOOL

Established by Anne Smith, a black teacher affectionately known by her former students as "Miss Anne," the school was named in honor of its founder's mother. It was located on or near Lyndon Avenue on the northwest side of Athens.

A graduate of Atlanta University, Anne Smith taught at Knox Institute and Heard University before starting her own school. "Her object was to care for a section of town not covered by the public schools, and to furnish a school where children who have to help their parents could attend at odd times."

The school maintained a relatively small enrollment in order to facilitate Miss Anne's individualized method of teaching. Although it contained a high school department, the Rosa Smith School offered no definite curriculum. Each student was given the opportunity to progress at his or her own speed, and was permitted to come to class whenever duties and chores were completed at home.

THE COUNTY SCHOOLS

Although not as well developed as their city counterparts, the black schools in rural Clarke County provided invaluable educational opportunities for children who lived nearby. Most of these schools were located near the various black churches which were scattered throughout the county.

In 1916 there were twenty-eight schools, equally distributed between blacks and whites, operating in rural Clarke County. The management of all but one of these institutions was in the hands of the county board of education, which was separate and distinct from the body that administered the Athens City School System. The schools were funded exclusively by the state of Georgia, with the exception of the Model and Training School, which received funds from private donors.

All the black county schools were located in one-room buildings except the Model and Training and Midway schools. The Billups Grove, Timothy, Allenville, and Brooklyn schools were housed in church buildings. In 1915 a Phelps-Stokes researcher stated that these four schools were among the poorest in Clarke County.

According to the same researcher, most of the school buildings were in poor condition and generally ill-equipped. The St. James school building on the Jefferson Road was "not well suited to school purposes." Classes at the Shiloh and Mount Sinai schools were held on the first floors of lodge buildings located on church grounds.

Rural county school for blacks

The following description of the schools was made in the *Rural Survey of Clarke County, Georgia*:

> The church schools are as unattractive within as they are from the outside. The blackboard facilities are wretched, and the frame benches are poor substitutes for desks. There are no pictures or maps in these schools, and few in most of the others. All the schools are heated with unjacketed stoves, some of which are in bad condition. Four of the buildings in use are in good condition, five in fair, five in bad condition, and three unfit for use as school houses.

The generally poor physical condition of the black county schools was due to several factors. Some of the schools were only in their first decades of existence, but all of them were crippled by discriminatory appropriations of educational funds under the "separate but equal" doctrine. Although black students accounted for 63 percent of the total county student population in 1916, the black schools received *only 33 percent* of the financial appropriations for that year.

Appropriation figures for the entire state are even more startling, During the 1929-30 school year, the racial composition of Georgia's public schools was 61 percent white and 39 percent black, but the white schools received *91 percent* of the total appropriation. Within this atmosphere, "a new roof, an uncontaminated well, a decent sanitary outhouse, and enough school books to go around were counted as solid accomplishments" by black teachers.

It was upon this scene that the Jeanes teachers and supervisors appeared in Georgia in 1907. The founder and original financial contributor to the program was Miss Anna T. Jeanes, a white woman of the Quaker faith who wanted to aid and improve rural black schools scattered throughout the South. Anna Jeanes' first effort in this direction was the placement of Jeanes teachers in counties in the southern states where one-teacher demonstration schools were established.

The first demonstration school was opened in Clarke County in 1932. Mrs. Quinton Jones was the first Jeanes supervisor employed by the county school board, followed by Miss Mamie Sapp Dye, Mrs. Mary Trawick, and Miss Madie Kincy. The success of the Jeanes supervision program in the black county schools prompted the Athens city school superintendent to hire Mrs. Ella Billups to serve as the Jeanes teacher in the black city schools in 1955.

Jeanes teachers were employed by local school boards throughout Georgia, and served as supervisors of rural black schools in each county. Through the efforts of these men and women, significant improvements in curricula, teaching methods, and physical facilities were made in black schools in Georgia and several other southern states.

Although the programs were unrelated, Jeanes supervisors and agricultural extension agents worked closely in Clarke County to improve the farming techniques of rural students and their parents. Through the establishment of 4-H Clubs in the schools, extension agents were able to organize farmer co-operatives, various group workshops, and stage community-wide agricultural fairs annually. Seven men served as county agents in the black communities of rural Clarke County: P.H. Stones, D.A. Starks, Edgar Cooper, Robert Church, Lloyd Trawick, E.R. Gary, and Herman Hackney.

Black male and female instructors were paid an average monthly salary of $24.00 and $23.45 respectively. White male instructors were paid an average monthly wage of $70.00, and white females earned an average pay of $48.20 per month. The monthly cost of tuition in the county school system averaged $2.40 for each white student and 73¢ per black student.

The following table offers a brief description of the fourteen black county schools. The map on page 84 shows the name and location of county schools and churches.

DESCRIPTION OF BUILDINGS, NEGRO SCHOOLS RURAL 1916

	Number of Rooms					Cloak Room		Painted		Desks		Play Grounds		Location		Flower Garden		General Conditions	
	1	2	3	4	5	Yes	No	Yes	No	Pat.	Not	Good	Poor	Good	Poor	Yes	No	Fair	Bad
Midway	•	•					•	•			•	•			•		•	•	
Oak Grove	•						•	•			•		•		•		•		•
Billups †	•						•		•		•		•	•			•		•
Morton's Chapel	•						•	•			•	•		•			•	•	
St. Luke's	•						•	•			•	•			•		•	•	
Allenville †	•						•		•		•		•		•		•		•
Timothy †	•						•		•		•		•		•		•		•
Chestnut Grove	•						•	•			•	•		•			•	•	
Mt. Sinai	•						•		•		•	•		•			•	•	
St. James	•						•		•		•		•		•		•	•	
Brooklyn †	•						•		•		•	•		•			•		•
Shiloh	•						•		•		•	•		•			•	•	
Model & Tr.			•			•		•			•	•		•		•		•	
Macedonia	•						•		•		•	•			•		•	•	
TOTAL	12	1	1			1	13	6	8		14	9	5	7	7	1	13	9	5

† in church buildings

JUDIA C. JACKSON HARRIS SCHOOL

As a rule, the county schools maintained relatively small enrollments and offered courses covering only the basic reading and writing skills. One notable exception to this rule was the Model and Training School, later renamed the Judia C. Jackson Harris School.

Along with the basic grammar and math courses, Harris School students were trained in art, music, and drama. On several occasions, students at the school presented musical pageants at the Morton Opera House in Athens. Judia Harris, founder of the school, wrote and produced at least four pageants which had racial, historical, and religious themes.

The institution was also the site of an annual agricultural fair, which drew large crowds from Clarke and surrounding counties. Canned goods, livestock, quilting, and other farm goods were exhibited, with prizes awarded to the best entries in each category.

The Harris School campus consisted of one three-room wooden structure serving as the main classroom facility, and a two-room home economics building. A fire of still unknown origin completely destroyed the three-room wooden building around 1926. However, classes continued to be held in the home economics building, and in Judia Harris' home which was located directly across the Danielsville Highway from the school.

Blacks and whites came to the aid of the Harris School after a drive to raise funds for the rebuilding of the structure was begun. White philanthropist Julius Rosenwald was the principal financial contributor. Rosenwald was the founder of the Rosenwald Fund, which contributed to the construction and improvement of over 6,000 rural Negro schools in the South.

By 1929, a four-classroom brick structure with a principal's office, library, and auditorium had been constructed on the school campus. A Phelps-Stokes Studies observer wrote:

> [The] Training School is the only Negro building in the county where the property is in good condition. The grounds are well kept and have flowers planted. ... The premises are kept clean of trash, and altogether presents a neat appearance.

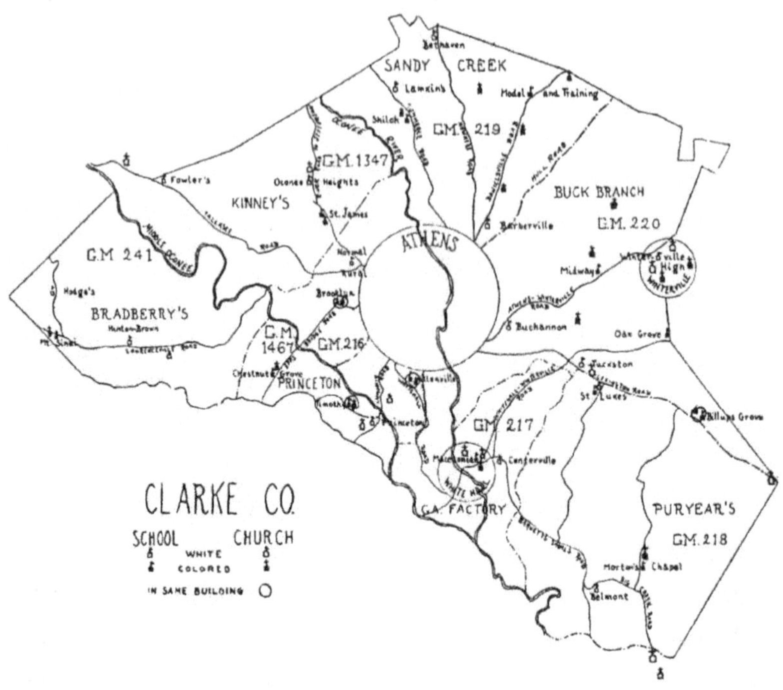

Map of Militia Districts, schools and churches in Clarke County

The school was founded in 1903 by Judia C. Jackson. She was born on February 1, 1873 in Athens to Alfred and Louise Jackson, graduated from Atlanta University in 1894, and received postgraduate instruction at Harvard College, the University of Chicago, and the University of Pennsylvania. In 1912 she became the second wife of Samuel F. Harris who was also a prominent local educator. Jackson held leadership positions in several local, state, and national organizations. She was the recipient of a Teacher's Life Certificate and a lithograph from the governor of Georgia in honor of her educational service to the state. In 1925, she authored and published a book entitled *Race Relations.*

Judia Jackson Harris devoted her entire career to the educational and social improvement of blacks in rural Clarke County. Because she espoused a philosophy of self-help and economic independence, she organized Land Owner Clubs in 1901. Their principal purposes were "to improve Negro home life and to establish a substantial school that should be the center of all activities."

Judia Harris and the Corn Club

Using the Model and Training School as a base, Harris helped develop the surrounding community and, according to one source, aided blacks in the purchase of "more than two thousand acres of land...."

> The first club contained ten members. They paid in $100 in cash in 1900 and obtained bond for title to a tract of forty acres (later increased to fifty-five acres), the purchase price being $350 for the forty acres. In 1908,... the tract was divided among the members...

During the next seven years, four other Land Owner or Corn Clubs were organized, and by 1915, the organizations had acquired a total of 440 acres valued at more than $3,000. Under the direction of Harris, the clubs expanded their cooperative investments and purchased a community sawmill, a cotton gin, and a threshing machine.

Apparently, there was a strong sense of competition between the city and county schools in Clarke County during the early part of the twentieth century. This competition often bordered on mutual contempt. Woofter notes that, in 1912, at least three of the county's black principals were not on speaking terms and seldom missed an opportunity to belittle the work of their counterparts in city or county.

There is little doubt that this discord influenced Harris to send her graduates to schools outside the city of Athens. But regardless of her motives, Harris School graduates successfully matriculated at prep, undergraduate, and graduate schools in all parts of the United States.

Because of failing health, Judia Harris retired in 1950 from the teaching profession and from the principalship of the school she had founded. Supported by the Slater Fund, the Phelps-Stokes Fund, by private donations, and by Clarke County, the school remained open until 1956 when the city and county school systems merged. Four years later, Judia Harris died at the age of eighty-seven. Today there is a nightclub on the spot where the main building of the Harris School campus was located.

THE CITY SCHOOLS

The movement that led to the establishment of a free public school system in Clarke County began around 1870, but the long-standing tradition of private education in Athens and surrounding areas impeded the birth of the public system for more than fifteen years.

Local opponents of public schools reasoned that the proposed system would create greater tax burdens. According to historian Augustus Hull, "the public school was a Massachusetts invention and we [Athenians] were becoming Yankeenized fast enough anyhow." Another historian, Robert Gamble, suggests that some local whites were also afraid that free schools for blacks "could lead to serious consequences for the social system which white Athenians wished to preserve...."

But there were others, black and white, who strongly supported the concept of "free schools for everybody." This group included black legislator Mat Davis, Emory Speer, a white attorney, and the editors of the two white newspapers. Speer addressed several of the university literary societies to extol the virtues of free public education. Representative Davis supported public education measures throughout his career in the legislature. The *Southern Watchman* also pleaded the cause of free schools to its Athens readers:

> It costs an average of three times as much for tuition in Athens, as the charge in the public schools of Savannah, Atlanta, Brunswick, or other places... We certainly have more than five thousand inhabitants ... and ... can establish a splendid system of free schools... Other towns and cities of the state have done this.... Let us not be behind in the race for knowledge.

Even before the establishment of Knox Institute in Athens, some blacks in the area benefited from educational instruction supplied by benevolent white masters. At the request of his former slaves, Colonel David Barrow built a school on his Oglethorpe County plantation and hired a white teacher to instruct forty black children in the fall of 1866. And although it violated Georgia law, Olivia Cobb tutored her girl-servant in the basics of reading, writing, and arithmetic.

> Olivia called her "a most excellent" domestic, but confessed that "more common sense and not quite so much genius" would make her a better servant. At any rate, the nurse progressed so rapidly under the tutelage

> that Olivia soon confessed to her husband that she felt "almost incompetent to teach her."

The first public schools opened in Athens in 1886. An application to establish the city-run schools was approved on October 15, 1885. It was signed by M.A. Harden, Clerk of the Georgia House of Representatives, William A. Little, Speaker of the House; H.A. Carlton, President of the Senate; and the Honorable D. McDaniel, Governor of Georgia.

In his annual report, Athens School Superintendent E.C. Branson recounted the board's initial efforts in the field of public education.

> Contending against a deep-rooted opposition to the public school idea, the Board of Education erected two, two-story, ten-roomed brick buildings, one for each race.

The school for black students was on Baxter Street, and the white school on Washington Street. Black children also used the Foundry Street, or Methodist School, which had four teachers. Mamie Jackson was principal in 1886. In 1890, A.J. Carey was made principal of Baxter Street School, which had six "well-trained Negro teachers."

The Baxter Street School was remodeled in 1893 for use by white students. The black students were moved to two six-room frame buildings on the east and west sides of Athens. Professor J.R. Mack was appointed principal of the smaller East Athens School, which was manned by a three-member faculty. A.J. Carey was given the principalship of the West Broad Street School which offered seven grades taught by five teachers. "Under Carey's management, the West Athens School increased in grades from seven to nine and became a high school."

Following a short tenure as principal of the East Athens School, Professor Samuel F. Harris (later husband of Judia Jackson Harris) was appointed principal of the West Broad Street School in 1903. The following year he designed and introduced into the curriculum an agricultural self-help program at the school, a garden to supply food for underprivileged students.

West Broad Public School for Negroes

Although the West Broad Street School was equipped with only the barest essentials, T.J. Woofter penned the following observation in 1912:

> Under conditions such as this it is hard to do any work of merit, and yet several unexpected visits to the school showed that the children were learning very well what was put before them.

Severe overcrowding at the east and west Athens schools was one of the major problems of early public education. Although black public school enrollment increased from 746 in 1893 to 1,004 in 1911, black students continued to attend classes taught by a total of fourteen instructors in two wood-frame buildings.

> Consequently, the little children could not be placed in school, and if they could have been, the schools were too crowded for them to have thorough instruction. The need of another Negro grade school became evident, and a four-room grade school was added in 1911-12, the corps of teachers being increased to 17.

However, the addition of the Newtown School did little to alleviate the overcrowded conditions at the West Broad Street School. During the 1912-13 school year, there was a total first grade enrollment of 140 with an average daily attendance of 105. This large number of students compelled one teacher to teach in split sessions, holding one section until 11:30 in the morning, then teaching a second until two in the afternoon.

In 1917, the Superintendent's Annual Report listed Professor Harris as principal of the Athens High and Industrial School (A.H.I.S.) built in 1913 on Reese Street, and as supervisor of all black schools in Athens. Professor Harris also taught tenth grade, while Mrs. Annie H. Burney taught eighth and ninth. In 1918, under Harris' supervision, evening vocational classes were added to the curriculum at A.H.I.S. Adults were "given the opportunity to learn cooking, sewing, home nursing, carpentry, masonry, and the rudiments of bookkeeping."

An eleventh grade was added in 1916, and in 1922 Athens High and Industrial became one of the first black public secondary schools to be accredited in the state of Georgia. Four years later, in 1926, Harris organized the state summer school for black teachers.

Mrs. Burney served for many years as assistant principal, and she took over as principal of the high school in 1934 when Professor Harris became seriously ill. He died the following year. Professor Aaron Brown succeeded him both as principal of A.H.I.S. and supervisor of black schools. Brown was an ardent believer in the necessity for extracurricular activities to promote the educational growth of economically and socially disadvantaged students. During his ten-year tenure as principal of A.H.I.S., Brown added several "extra-class activities" to the school's program. They were:

(left to right) Rufus Sims, Chester Davenport, James Whitehead, E.T. "Doc" Holmes and Homer T. Edwards worked to restore the original Athens High and Industrial School building, which opened in 1914.

> ...the Athletic Association, whose purpose was to train girls and boys to be great athletes; Debating Club, to stimulate interest in the conclusion of problems; Dramatic Club, to train students who are more interested in dramatization; Glee Club, to train students who are interested in singing; Tri-Hi-Y and Hi-Y, to create, maintain and extend throughout the school and community high standards of Christian character.

Professor Charles Duvaul succeeded Brown in 1938. He was followed by Homer T. Edwards, Sr. eight years later. Professor Edwards recalls one of his most gratifying experiences as a local educator: being able to move into the new high school building on Dearing Street in 1956. Professor Edwards retired in 1968 and was succeeded by E.T. Roberson.

In 1964 a group composed of students, teachers, and parents spearheaded a movement to have the black high school's name changed. Following approval by the Clarke County Board of Education, Athens High and Industrial School was renamed Burney-Harris High School in honor of two black educators, Annie H. Burney and Samuel F. Harris.

Meanwhile, hundreds of miles to the north in our nation's capital, an event occurred which drastically changed the nature of public education in Athens and the rest of the country. In the spring of 1954, in the landmark case of *Brown v. Board of Education of Topeka*, the United States Supreme Court ruled that "separate but equal" public education was an illegal, un-workable doctrine. The following year, the high court ordered that its desegregation ruling should be carried out with "all deliberate speed."

In the years following the Supreme Court's desegregation ruling, Georgia politicians enacted statutes and instituted policies designed to frustrate any attempt to integrate the state's public school system. In fact, in the spring of 1956, the Georgia attorney general stated that he would seek enactment of a law that would make it "a capital crime for any public official in Georgia" to enforce federal desegregation rulings. In the fall of 1954, Governor-elect Marvin Griffin proclaimed, "Come hell or high water, the races will not be mixed in Georgia!" A few months later, the governor and the legislature were given the constitutional power to "abolish the public schools and create a system of private schools" if the federal courts ordered the state-supported schools to integrate.

In December of 1955, Governor Griffin attempted to persuade the state Board of Regents to prohibit state-supported colleges from "playing with a non-segregated sports team or before a non-segregated audience."

The following year, the state parks director announced that nine Georgia parks would be leased to private citizens in order to avoid court orders demanding desegregation of public facilities.

Two years later, in 1958, Governor Griffin vowed to close the public schools in Atlanta rather than allow them to be integrated. Griffin's successor in the Governor's Mansion, Ernest Vandiver, continued the battle against integration by pledging to preserve segregation. In July of 1958, he "hired a special team of lawyers" and instructed them to discover ways to defeat court-ordered desegregation. Finally, the Georgia Legislature voted to cut off funding to any state-supported institution that integrated its student body.

Although these and other efforts would temporarily dam the tide of integration in Georgia, the onrushing pressures of the 1960s Civil Rights movement would first crack and then topple the walls of segregation. The first blows were struck against segregated public education in Georgia in Athens at the University of Georgia in January 1961. The admission of Charlayne Hunter and Hamilton Holmes, two black Atlanta natives, to the university and the resulting student unrest brought national attention to the school, the city, and the state.

Political and civil rights observers quickly realized that the shaded and generally peaceful campus had become a major legal and social battleground. It would witness the head-on collision of what was quickly becoming the irresistible force of integration against the seemingly immovable object of segregation in the State of Georgia.

Hunter and Holmes, both possessing outstanding academic records, applied for admission as transfer students to the University of Georgia early in 1960. After considering their applications, the university's admissions director wrote Charlayne Hunter informing her "that she would be considered for admission the following fall" because there would be no dormitory space available for transfer students until then. Holmes was told that he "had been 'evasive' in answering the questions put to him by the three-man panel" which interviewed him.

In the subsequent discrimination trial brought by the two students, the registrar testified that the "evasiveness" charge stemmed from Holmes' negative reply to a question as to whether or not he had ever been arrested. Registrar William Danner told the court the admissions office had information which showed that Holmes had "once been fined and had had his license suspended for speeding." Because of this, Holmes' application for admission was denied.

The two prospective students then filed a discrimination suit against the university charging that they were being denied admission to the school solely on the basis of their race. They were represented in the case by a team of civil rights lawyers which included Donald Hollowell of Atlanta and Constance Baker Motley of the National Association for the Advancement of Colored People (NAACP) Legal Defense Fund. (In 1966 Mrs. Motley was appointed judge of the Federal Circuit Court for the Southern District of New York.)

After a week-long trial, which began in December in the federal courthouse in Athens, and in which many of the university's highest officials testified, Judge William Bootle issued his historic decision. On January 6 in Macon he wrote:

> Although there is no written policy or rule excluding Negroes, including the plaintiffs, from admission to the university on account of their race and color, there is a tacit policy to that effect...

The judge concluded that Hamilton Holmes and Charlayne Hunter "would already have been admitted had it not been for their race or color."

Although the decision in favor of the plaintiffs had been more or less expected by political observers, one portion of the order caught litigants on both sides of the issue totally by surprise. Judge Bootle also ruled that the two black students should be allowed to enter the university, but not the following fall or the spring quarter beginning in March. Hunter and Holmes could begin attending classes during the winter quarter. This decision, rendered on a cold Friday afternoon in January, gave the victorious plaintiffs just two days to prepare for winter quarter registration scheduled for the following Monday.

Registration and the first three days of classes for the black students were uneventful and generally peaceful, prompting television newscasters and northern newspapermen to compliment university officials and students on their good behavior. But there were catcalls, grim stares from passersby and, in Charlayne Hunter's case, groups of students who followed her around campus. At one point, white students surrounded the car she was riding in and began to bounce it.

According to Calvin Trillin, an Atlanta newspaper reporter, the students were more "playful" than menacing. But their playful nature quickly dissipated in the wake of the violence that occurred on the night of January 11. Throughout the day, three law students busied themselves organizing what would evolve into a widely publicized racial incident at the University of Georgia.

According to one source, it had become more or less general knowledge by the afternoon that a riot was scheduled to occur in front of Charlayne Hunter's dormitory after the Georgia-Georgia Tech basketball game. Some students reportedly "got dates for the basketball game and the riot afterwards."

> Just after ten, a small crowd of students gathered on the lawn in front of Center Myers and unfurled a bed sheet bearing the legend "Nigger Go Home." Then three or four of them peeled off from the group, ran toward the dormitory, and flung bricks and Coke bottles through the window of Charlayne's room—the mob grew to about a thousand people, many of them throwing bricks, rocks and firecrackers.

The disturbance was finally quelled by the arrival of Dean William Tate and a group of Athens policemen. Tate ordered the students to leave the area and began confiscating the identification cards of those who refused to follow his commands. Meanwhile the policemen retaliated against some students who had been pushing them by firing tear gas into the group of students.

The short-lived incident left the area around Center Myers Hall with the appearance of a deserted battlefield. Bricks and broken glass littered the lawn, small brush fires burned in the woods below the dormitory, and the stifling smell of tear gas hung in the air. There were several casualties including, as Trillin observes, the university's reputation. Holmes and Hunter were almost immediately dismissed from school by the dean of students for their "own safety and the safety of almost seven thousand other students...." The two students were then driven back to Atlanta by Georgia state troopers.

The Wednesday night racial disturbance sent shock waves throughout the state and nation. Holmes and Hunter received hundreds of letters in admiration of their "courage and dignity" in the face of racial hostilities. A majority of Georgia's political leaders expressed dismay over the disturbance and criticized the violent tactics of the students. University of Georgia faculty members met the night after the disturbance. About four hundred of them eventually signed a resolution insisting that "the two suspended students be returned to their classes."

Governor Ernest Vandiver officially guaranteed that order would be maintained, and following the issuance of a new court order, the black students returned to campus the following Monday. Their matriculation at the institution continued undisturbed for approximately two-and-one-half years until both students graduated in 1963.

Trillin wrote that the admission of Holmes and Hunter to the university "was the turning point for Georgia, and was accomplished in a way and at a time that made it inevitable that the state would move forward... And according to Donald Hollowell, one of the black attorneys who represented the plaintiffs in the university desegregation suit, it was "the case that turned the state around and allowed them to start, or at least see what was in the other direction."

In 1968, Athenian Maxie Elliot Foster became the first black to attend UGA on an athletic scholarship. In 1972, he became captain of the track team, another first. Between receiving his bachelor's and his master's from the University of Georgia, he returned to Clarke Central High School, which he had previously attended under the "freedom of choice" integration plan, as a coach.

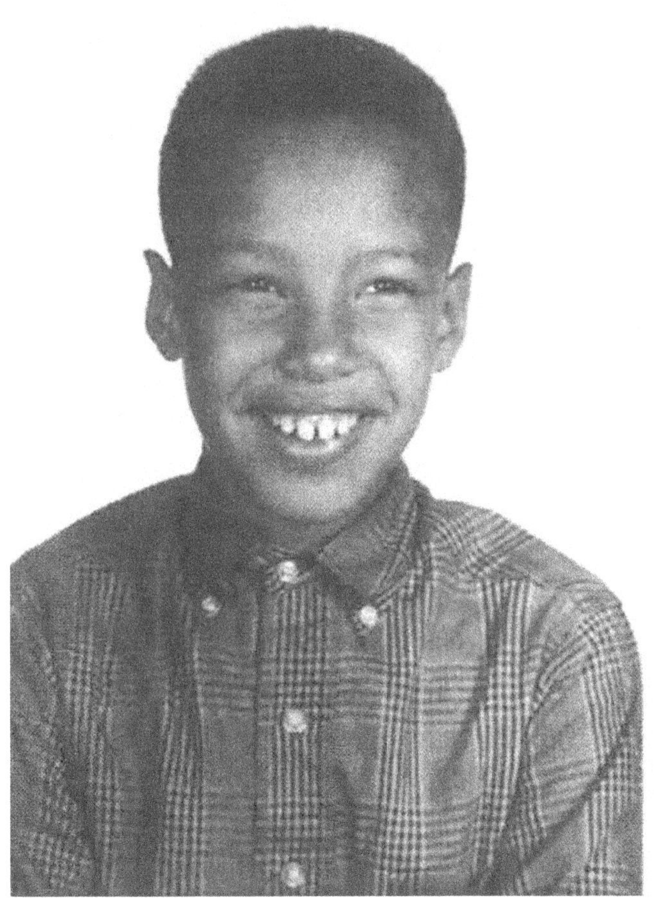

Scott Michael Killian integrated third grade at Chase Street School

Through the 1960s, the tide of integration pushed across the state of Georgia. The trickle that began in Athens gained strength and magnitude as it journeyed on its uncertain course. Georgia Tech was integrated in the fall of 1961. The following year, five black children integrated the Atlanta public school system.

On September 2, 1963, under the school board's "freedom of choice" plan, four black girls—Wilucia Green, her sister Marjorie Green, Agnes Green (no relation), and Bonnie Hampton—and one boy, Scott Michael Killian, became the first members of their race to attend the previously all-white schools in Clarke County. They integrated three different schools, accompanied each day by a parent or local pastor, and local newspapers said little about the event, except to announce that there were no crowds around the schools. Although angry whites had rioted at the University of Georgia two years earlier following the admission of two blacks, the desegregation of Clarke's public schools was not marred by mass protest or violence.

However, black students were subjected to verbal abuse, ostracism, and intimidation by some of their white classmates. Majorie Green, Agnes Green and Bonnie Hampton were placed in separate units at Child Street School, which was the seventh-grade school for all white students. In a letter dated September 3, 1963, addressed to Miss Rosa Strickland, a former instructor, Margie wrote about her "unique" situation and expressed her hopes for the future.

> I was sitting in a classroom of 33 children, all the opposite race. I used to sit and watch older people shake because of nervous conditions, and now I was experiencing the same thing. The girls that were sitting in front of me turned around and smiled but no one said anything. When I went to lunch I had to sit by a person who didn't especially like Negroes. He moved over...as far as it has gone it is alright, and I think it is going to be fine in the future.

Wilucia Green attended Athens High School (now Clarke Central), and Scott Killian was the lone black third grader at Chase Street Elementary School. For the next six years, other African-American students elected to attend the white schools, in small numbers. In the late 1960s, a small number of black teachers were sent to white schools, and white teachers to black. The first black teachers to be assigned to the all-white schools in Clarke County were: Johnnie Lay Burks, Chase Street Elementary School, Bettye Henderson Holston, Alps Road Elementary School, Victoria Baker Stroud, Barnett Shoals Elementary School, Jeanette Browning, Clarke Middle School and Ruth Hawk Payne, Athens High School.

(left to right) Marjorie Green, Judge James Barrow, Donald Hollowell, Bonnie Hampton, Wilucia Green and Agnes Green at a September 6,1992 ceremony celebrating school integration at Hill Chapel Baptist Church

Finally, after a decade and a half of exercising "deliberate speed" in carrying out the high court's desegregation mandate, local school officials acknowledged the inevitable. They pre-pared to totally merge the separate school systems in the fall of 1970. During the year that preceded the merger, biracial committees were formed to facilitate a smooth, orderly transition. But history would ultimately record that the chasms that had been created by decades of racial segregation would not be easily traversed.

Negotiations between blacks and whites at Burney-Harris and Athens high schools progressed slowly or not at all during the spring of 1970. Clarence Pope, a rising senior at Burney-Harris during that eventful spring, recalls that the negotiations were aggravated by distrust and apprehension. "It looked as if Burney-Harris and everything that was associated with it was going to be swallowed up in the merger. We had everything to lose and nothing to gain," Pope said.

Pope echoed the sentiments of many Burney-Harris students who wanted equal education but did not wish to lose their identity or the identity of their school in the process of achieving it. While they might have agreed that Athens High School had the larger building and was therefore the more logical place to house the newly integrated student body, they did not want to adopt the school's name, principal, faculty, colors, team mascot, or newspaper in the bargain. The situation was further complicated by the intense athletic rivalry between the two schools.

Eventually the high school was given a new name (Clarke Central High School); the Burney-Harris Highlight and the Athens High *Thumbtack Tribune* became the *Highlights of the Thumbtack Tribune*; the new school colors, red and gold, combined Burney-Harris' blue and gold with Athens High's red and white; and Clarke Central's athletes became the Gladiators instead of Trojans or Yellow Jackets. The school retained a white principal, but some black teachers from Burney-Harris taught at Clarke Central. Leaders of both schools shared leadership of the integrated student body.

Meanwhile, black students at both schools were frustrated. On the morning of April 16, 1970, angry black students from Burney-Harris and

Athens High carried their protests and frustrations into the streets of the city. There was violence and vandalism at both high school campuses.

Late that afternoon, Superior Court Judge James Barrow issued an injunction restraining thirteen named students and John Doe One Through One Hundred "from any acts which might interrupt normal school operations." The injunction also ordered the named defendants "to show cause at 11 a.m., April 27 ... why they should not be temporarily enjoined as spelled out in the restraining order."

Burney-Harris Principal E.T. Roberson and Athens High Principal Don Hight reconstructed the events that led to the issuance of the injunction. Roberson told a local reporter that a group of male students assembled in the downstairs corridor at the Burney-Harris building before the first period class change. After some discussion, they moved their meeting outside the building to an area near the entrance to the school gymnasium.

Roberson and Coach E.T. Holmes talked briefly with the students, instructing them to either return to class or leave the school grounds. The group of approximately 150 refused to reenter the school and departed for Athens High.

Racial troubles were also brewing at Athens High, which through "freedom of choice" now had 120 black students out of a total enrollment of nearly 1,600. Nathaniel Fox, a black senior, recalls trouble first breaking out after two black students were left on the bench at a basketball game. "They came out of the locker room after halftime dressed (in street clothes) and walked across the court making the clenched fist sign in protest. Outside, words were exchanged, fights broke out. It was a powder keg."

Several days later, on April 16, when the school day opened at the predominantly white school "a large number of black students were gathered in the lobby of the auditorium" discussing a newspaper story "dealing with efforts to ease racial tension at the school." The students were upset about statements in the article and the overall racial situation at Athens High, according to Don Hight.

> [He asked] the students to go to their classes, as did Assistant Principal Walter Allen and teacher, Mrs. Clara Gay. A majority of them did so... but some of them remained and wanted to discuss further the article and other situations.

While talking with the remaining students, Hight received a call from Principal Roberson informing him that a group of students from Burney-Harris were enroute to his school. When they heard that the Burney-Harris students were in the vicinity of their campus, the black students and some white supporters from Athens High joined the Burney-Harris students in the auditorium parking lot.

Athens police officers arrived on the scene as Hight and Roberson conferred with student leaders on the steps leading to the E.B. Mell Auditorium. The discussions quickly reached an impasse and were broken off. The black students then rushed the Athens High building and broke through the police guards into the school.

Several white students were attacked, Assistant Principal Allen was "struck in the back several times," one student was hit in the face with a baseball bat, and several black Athens High students "who were attempting to restore order" were also beaten. Alphonzo Lawrence was among the Burney-Harris students that morning. "It was strange," he recalled. "There was hate in the eyes of many of the students. The things we did were wrong but we were so frustrated ... and so young."

Local police restored order at the school within twenty to twenty-five minutes. The black students then returned to the Burney-Harris campus where some of the students "smashed flowerpots, discharged fire extinguishers, knocked out windows, and broke glass panels in doors," according to Principal Roberson.

The following day, Athens High and Burney-Harris were placed under police guard in an effort to curb any further disturbances. A large group of Burney-Harris students met across the street from the main entrance of the Burney-Harris building and refused to enter the school in protest against the presence of the policemen and the issuance of the restraining order.

At approximately 9 a.m., student leaders requested an audience with Clarke County School Superintendent Dr. Charles P. McDaniel. A meeting which lasted about an hour was held in the school gymnasium with McDaniel "answering questions and trying to help them understand the situation." McDaniel concluded the meeting by telling the students that "we will continue to maintain the police ... as long as they are needed" to insure that "those who want to go to school have the opportunity to do so..."

Racial turmoil and high absenteeism continued to plague the county high schools for more than a week, as local education leaders, parents, and teachers sought solutions to the problems precipitated by the planned school merger. Throughout the spring and summer, meetings and negotiations continued between the interested parties. The April disturbances had proven that a great deal of work remained to be done before the September merger deadline.

Finally, the doors of the county's public schools swung open at the beginning of the 1970 fall term amid the fears of some and the hopes of others. After eighty-four years of racial separation, the two systems were totally merged, and a new day dawned for public education in Clarke County, Georgia.

Integration brought new problems. Within a few years, schools in traditionally black neighborhoods were phased out. The buildings were converted to use for administration or special programs, instead of as schools, and traditionally African American neighborhoods lost their community focus. There was pressure, real or perceived, on black educators to leave the system, and there were fewer administrative positions for blacks.

By 1974, according to the *Athens Voice*, the number of African-American instructors had dropped from 113 (in 1969) to 95, while the number of white instructors had grown from 333 to 364. During the same years, the number of black students grew from 3,554 to 3,889. White enrollment dropped by nearly 700 students, from 7,293 to 6,609.

As for administrators of the consolidated black and white systems, Howard Stroud continued as principal of Lyons Middle School, and W.H. McBride in 1974 became the first principal of a formerly all-white school, Clarke Middle School. In 1975, McBride was moved to an assistant principalship at Clarke Central, and Milton Hill became principal at formerly white Barrow Elementary School.

More than a decade passed before Russell Studevan became principal of Clarke Central High School. In 1995 Charles Worthy became principal of Cedar Shoals High School. Also in 1995, Dr. Lucian Harris became the first black superintendent of schools, serving until 2000. Both Ernest Hardaway and Howard Stroud served as assistant superintendents, and as interim superintendents between permanent superintendents.

The African-American community continued to press to have more of their race in administrative position, and fought to regain strengths lost in the transition, such as its neighborhood schools. Fourth Street School, opened in 1990, brought a community elementary school back into the east Athens community.

African Americans also fought to keep the names of educators Samuel Harris, Annie Burney and C. H. Lyons on the county's school buildings. When Lyons Middle School closed, the former African-American high school, Burney-Harris, became Burney-Harris-Lyons middle school.

In 1995, the high school building on Dearing Street Extension ceased to be a school entirely, and was renamed the Homer T. Edwards Building. The name Burney-Harris-Lyons is perpetuated today in a middle school on Tallassee Road.

Today, 57 percent of Clarke County public school students are African American, but only 22 percent of their instructors are black, stated Mike Wooten, public relations director for the Board of Education. The number of black and white principals is approximately equal.

40th Anniversary Update

Dr. Demond Means is an enthusiastic educator who has devoted more than two decades helping students reach their full potential. Renowned as a national leader in closing achievement gaps, Dr. Means began as superintendent of the Clarke County School District on July 10, 2017.

As the superintendent, Dr. Means has prioritized improving academic growth through a relentless commitment to educational equity. Previously, he was the superintendent of the Mequon-Thiensville School District in Mequon, Wis., which was recognized as the best K-12 school district with an enrollment of 3,000 or more in Wisconsin by the state accountability system report card for three consecutive years. Consistent success led to being tapped as the chair of Wisconsin's Promoting Excellence for All – a task force formed by the Wisconsin Department of Instruction to develop strategies to address the state's achievement gap. Prior to that, Dr. Means was an assistant superintendent in the same school district, co-interim superintendent of the Wauwatosa School District in Wauwatosa, Wis., director of human resources for the Wauwatosa School District, principal of Maple Dale Middle School in Fox Point, Wis., assistant principal of Nicolet High School in Glendale, Wis. and a social studies teacher at Homestead High School in Mequon. Dr. Means earned three degrees including a bachelor's degree in secondary education from Concordia University, in addition to both a master's degree in educational administration and a doctorate in educational leadership from Cardinal Stritch University. In 2015, he completed the American Association of School Administrators National Superintendent Certification Program.

WHO ARE WE?

A Photo Essay

WHO ARE WE?

We are the pain and suffering of Mother Africa.
Torn from her womb we arrived in the "Land of the Free"
locked in chains. Orphaned and forsaken, we began
our sojourn in the wilderness of American slavery.

WHO ARE WE?

We are the tillers of soil and the hewers of wood.
King Cotton rose to power because we bent our backs in toil.
Our blood and tears have irrigated every inch of this fair land.
We are reapers of a bitter fruit.

WHO ARE WE?

We are singers of spirituals and conveyors of silent prayers.
Our unwavering faith was the beacon that guided us
through the long night of oppression.
Praying black hands fashioned hope
out of the bleak substance of despair.

Pitt McWhorter

WHO ARE WE?

We are schools and churches
built with the splintered blocks of American slavery.
Nurtured by faith and genius,
we made a way out of no way.
We are the common denominators of all things.
We are black letters in a white alphabet.

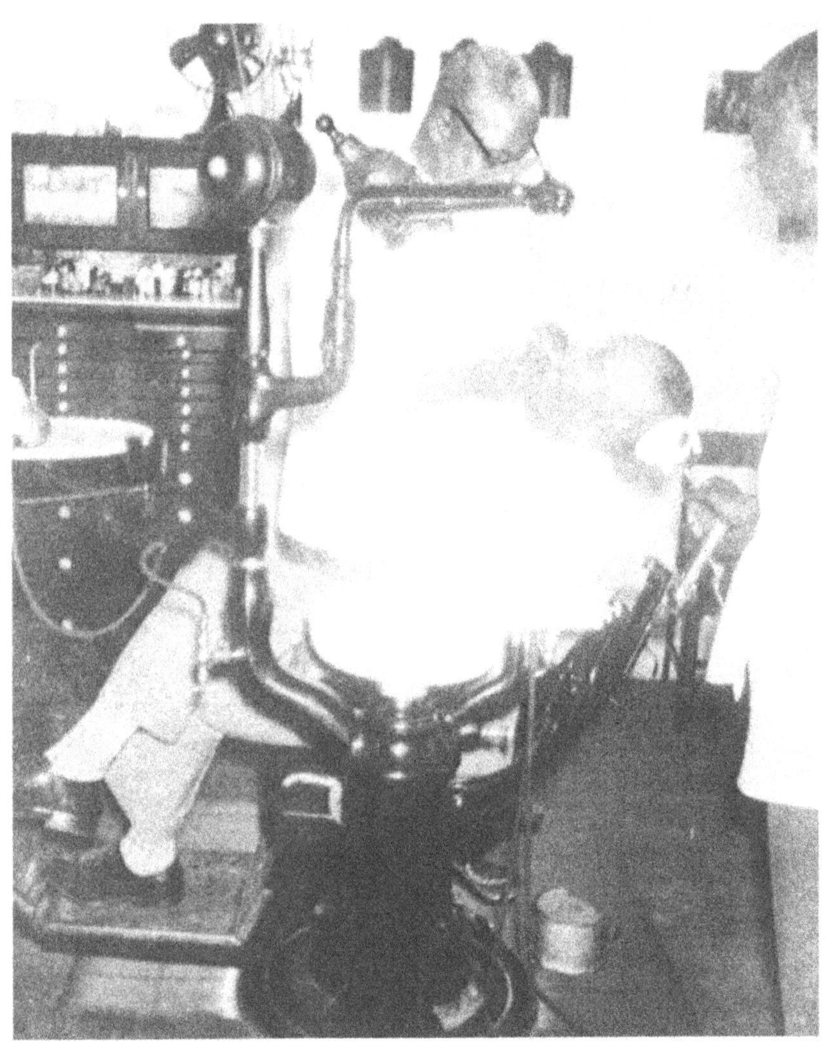

WHO ARE WE?

We are the sound of happy feet,
doing the Hustle and the Boogaloo!
Brave, black men march off to war---never to return.
On strong, swift legs we score game-winning touchdowns.
Our weary, defeated bodies
limp from arenas and playing fields.

Horace King

WHO ARE WE?

We are nameless faces—the heroes and heroines.
We are young and old,
We are teachers, preachers, healers and builders.
We are poor, illiterate and weak.
We are the fated children of poverty and wealth.

Alice Horam Wimberly and kindergarten class

WHO ARE WE?

We are the hope that springs eternal.
We have woven the thread of humanity
throughout the fabric of history.
Our dreams, though often deferred,
have not been destroyed.

GEORGIA
IT IS TIME

WHO ARE WE?

We are dark yesterdays and bright tomorrows.
We are all that is, was and shall be.
We are the boundless realm of human potential.
Who Are We???
My People—We Are!

MLT
Revised 2018

Samuel F. Harris

SAMUEL F. HARRIS

Educational Pioneer

I want to help my people
into work not out of it.
I want to teach the dignity of work…

SAMUEL F. HARRIS

The history of Athens is filled with the sacrifices and accomplishments of men and women who devoted their lives to the educational improvement of northeast Georgians. Professor Samuel F. Harris must be credited as one of the most outstanding of these dedicated educators and administrators.

Harris was in the vanguard of those who laid the foundation for the public school system in Clarke County. He was the first educator in the county and one of the first in Georgia to incorporate vocational and industrial training into the traditional public school curriculum.

In 1922, during his tenure as principal, Athens High and Industrial School became the first black public secondary school to be accredited in Georgia. Four years later, in 1926, Harris organized the State Summer School for black teachers at the University of Georgia. This unprecedented educational initiative gave black teachers from around the state the opportunity to gain valuable instruction from university faculty members.

Samuel Frederick Harris was born in Athens on February 3, 1875, the son of Henrietta Harris and an unidentified father. Harris was named for his grandfather, a talented shoemaker and a slave owned by a wealthy Athens family. His mother was a skilled seamstress and nurse, but she could not afford to send her son to the local black private schools. Instead, he received his early formal education in the public schools. During his youth, Harris gained the reputation of being a musical prodigy. His training was limited to occasional lessons from local black musicians and a Dr. Fischer, a white music instructor at the Lucy Cobb Institute. He quickly developed into a popular pianist and organist in the black community. Later, Harris performed at the Jewish Synagogue, the Presbyterian Church and the Colonial Opera House.

According to contemporary sources, the precocious young student also benefited from instruction by several prominent white professors, W.D. Hooper, H.C. White, and R.L. McWhorter of the University of Georgia and D.L. Earnest of the State Normal School. According to the wife of John D. Moss, a Harris benefactor, he "showed the ingenuity born of strong purpose" by learning to work Professor Earnest's classroom projector and, she wrote, "making his presence essential, and thus preventing any possibility of prejudice." Harris' daughter, Sarah Cureton, stated that her father excelled in his studies and was eventually allowed to tutor white students.

Although his skin color disqualified him from officially enrolling at the University of Georgia, Harris completed all graduation requirements. Despite intense lobbying from some local whites, college officials refused to grant him a degree. Mary Bondurant Warren, the great-niece of John D. Moss, recalled that local business leaders contributed money to a fund to send Harris to Morris Brown College in Atlanta. In 1903, the college awarded him a Master of Arts degree "based on his studies" at the University of Georgia. Later in his career, he studied at Harvard University and the University of Chicago. According to his obituary, printed in the Athens Banner-Herald on July 2, 1935, Harris "was pursuing the degree of Doctor of Philosophy at the University of Georgia when illness forced his retirement from school work."

The respected educator began his 38-year career in 1896, when he was hired to teach the second grade at the West Athens School (West Broad Street School). He and three other teachers earned $270 a year teaching in the four-room wood frame structure. The following year Harris was transferred to the East Athens School, which also had a faculty of four, including an attractive young teacher named Magnolia Randolph. Romance blossomed and the two educators were married in 1899. This was Harris' second marriage; the first to Nannie Frank of Albany was tragic and short-lived. Nannie Harris died a few months after they exchanged vows.

Following the death of his second wife, Harris married Judia C. Jackson in 1912. Jackson was born in Athens on February 1, 1873, and was graduated from Atlanta University in 1894. She received postgraduate instruction at Harvard University, the University of Pennsylvania and the University of Chicago. In 1903 Jackson founded the Model and Training School located on the Danielsville Highway. While her husband worked in the city schools, Judia Harris devoted her entire career to the educational and social improvement of rural Clarke County blacks. (See Chapter 4)

After returning to West Broad School as its principal in 1903, Harris discovered that only five percent of the students were completing the literary courses offered in the public schools. At the same time, he noted that there was "a general desertion of a class of domestic workers of their occupation," in the Athens area. The next year, believing a garden would supply food for underprivileged students, Harris started a garden and assigned small patches to each student. The adventure was so successful that the following year he rented ten acres of land, bought a horse and some agricultural tools and received an appropriation from the board of education to employ an agricultural graduate from Tuskegee Institute.

But his experiment was hampered by a general lack of interest among white school officials, and by inadequate funding. The small amount of money appropriated to the black schools in Athens could not be diverted to support industrial training, so Harris's vocational initiatives were primarily sustained by private donations. Hoping to expand the programs, he enlisted the aid of three local black men and went on a singing tour through the North to raise funds. The "quartette met discouragement, speaking, praying, and often singing of 'Home, Sweet Home,' with no certain place to lay their weary heads ..." wrote Mrs. John D. Moss. Although the tour was a financial failure, Harris returned to Athens determined to expand the availability of industrial and agricultural training in Athens.

Judia Jackson Harris

He convinced school officials to offer courses in cooking, sewing and agriculture, to be supported primarily by contributions. During 1908, ninety-eight black women attended Cooking Extension School classes, which met twice a week for six weeks. They were taught how to prepare various foodstuffs, their protein values, and their relation to good health. However, Harris realized it would be impossible to adequately cultivate vocational and moral ideals under such limited conditions. He became convinced that manual training could be provided, but "real industrial values and vocational direction need[ed] an environment where work is the constant ideal."

These observations led the ambitious young educator to develop plans for the construction of a practical school for the training of workers. He decided to build a vocational school that would offer courses in housekeeping, cooking, nursing, laundering, sewing, practical farming and the trades.

In September 1909, Harris met with four black men, the Rev. W.A. Gilham, Simon Pope, Moses G. Gilham, and David Hawkins, to discuss the nature and quality of education black students were receiving in the public school system. They agreed that children's education was not of a "useful character." A movement to establish a private industrial school was inaugurated, and before the meeting was over, $350 was raised to support the venture.

The men opened a vocational night school and quickly enrolled sixty-eight students. Three of the four men who helped Harris found the school taught trades to the boys. Girls and women were instructed in the domestic sciences. The night school was supported by an auxiliary board of women, most of them the wives of the five directors of the institution. According to Harris, teachers were hired to instruct students in literary work, carpentry, bricklaying, plastering and cooking.

Although little written material exists describing the social and educational philosophies of Samuel Harris, the few available documents suggest his beliefs were similar to those of Dr. Booker T. Washington, founder of Tuskegee Institute. During the twenty-year period that followed Washington's historic Cotton Exposition address in 1895, "the sage of Tuskegee" was the most influential black man in America. Washington believed blacks could improve their situation by educating themselves, and by becoming more efficient industrial or domestic workers. Basic to the Washingtonian philosophy was the idea that blacks should first strive to achieve economic parity (rather than political and social equality) with American whites. Once economic parity was achieved, Washington argued, whites would be willing to grant American Negroes limited political rights that did not violate the segregated social order.

Vocational night school cooking class

In a prospectus for his vocational school, Harris explained that courses at the institution would be designed "to meet the needs, primarily of the workers and not particularly those who want to prepare to be teachers or leaders." He and his local black supporters believed this type of education would "help save the great number of idle boys and girls from crime and ruined lives." Harris also noted that virtually none of the all-black educational institutions at that time were preparing their graduates to enter the agricultural and industrial job markets. Another common aspect of Washington's and Harris's plans for educating the masses of young blacks in the South was the enlistment of wealthy whites to finance their educational programs.

After enlisting support from the black community, Harris arranged a meeting with influential white educators, business-men and leaders from around the state. They included: H.S. West, judge of the City Court of Athens; David C. Barrow, chancellor of the University of Georgia; E.R. Hodgson, president of Empire State Chemical Company; John D. Moss, president of Moss Cotton Company; John E. Talmadge, Sr., president of Talmadge Mills and Wholesale Grocery Company; T.R. Vincent, vice president of Georgia National Bank; Billups A. Phinizy, president of Southern Mutual Insurance Company; William T. Bryan, president of Athens Electric Railway Company, and Judge John J. Strickland. Bryan, Talmadge, and Moss were elected to serve on an all-white board of trustees for the school, along with Robert F. Maddox, former mayor of Atlanta, C.J. Hood, president of the Northeastern Bank of Commerce; and H.H. Dean, an attorney from Gainesville, Georgia. The "Board of Colored Directors" included the original black supporters and A.T. Chunn, Moses Milner, L. Hunt, and Jackson Spalding.

Chancellor Barrow suggested the school be established as a memorial to the faithful "black Mammies" of the antebellum South. Harris apparently seized upon this nostalgia for the "old South" as an excellent way to raise funds from wealthy white contributors. At any rate, the proposed school was actually given two different names, The Black Mammy Memorial Institute and the Peace Monument. In its original brochure, Harris wrote:

> Conspicuous among the women who were eagerly pursuing this course in cooking were many of the "Old Black Mammies." This suggested that since this was the work in which the "old Mammies of the South" made

> themselves beloved and respected by the generations before the war, a befitting thing would be to name the school for them…

On September 19, 1910, the school's board of trustees petitioned the Superior Court of Clarke County for a twenty-year charter for the Black Mammy Memorial. Paragraph six of the petition stated that the purpose of the institute was to prepare young blacks "for the practical duties of life by training them for domestic service, and for service in the arts and trades..." A short time later, the City of Athens donated $2,000 and a twenty-five-acre tract of land in east Athens that was valued at $5,000. The trustees then issued an appeal for $25,000 for construction of Memorial Industrial Hall and two dormitories. Information concerning the project spread quickly throughout the state of Georgia. Former Georgia Governor W.J. Northern commended Harris for his effort "to establish an INDUSTRIAL school as a MEMORIAL to the Black Mammies of the South." *The Industrial Index of Georgia and Alabama* endorsed the project and volunteered its cooperation in the future.

The *Atlanta Constitution* printed a lengthy editorial supporting the establishment of the industrial school in Athens. The editors noted that the school would provide training, for "the great mass of negroes, and not for the exceptionally bright ones."

> It is not the aim of the institution to restrain nor discourage the production of leaders for the race, but it is the specific task and purpose of the "Black Mammy Memorial Institute" to raise the industrial and moral standard of the workers who constitute the rank and file of the race. The moral effort of this institution is to train its students to a deeper sense of the merits of a reliable, intelligent and consecrated life in the service for which they are best fitted. It is refreshing to note that the prospective institution will be founded and operated along these constructive lines.

But the white support for the project was probably based on reasons other than mere reverence for the idealized notion of faithful black mammies. Employers understood that skilled black industrial and agricultural workers would increase the productivity of their fields and factories. More importantly, Harris convinced his white supporters that the graduates of his institute, the "average Negroes," would not pose a threat to southern political and social systems based on the myth of white superiority.

Memorial Industrial Hall (as planned)

Harris clearly recognized the importance of securing financial support from the white community, and he tried to appease potential white contributors by advocating the training of blacks for "the practical duties of life." However, it is interesting to note that the institute's prospectus also contained an inconspicuous reference to academic training. Several non-industrial courses were listed, including English, "Common School Studies," Bible, hygiene, chemistry, and Morals. This might suggest that Harris, like the majority of his white supporters, may have harbored ulterior motives regarding the establishment of the Black Mammy Memorial Institute.

By 1911, the *Athens Daily Herald* reported that, "Athens has one institution, the like of which is not to be found anywhere else in the world." Although the proposed Memorial Industrial Hall had not been constructed, classes in housekeeping, cooking, nursing, laundering, sewing, practical farming, and the trades were taught in temporary facilities. The editors added: "No institution for the uplift of the Negro race and for his education in proper channels has more thorough sympathy on the part of the white people of the state than this. This fact in itself is an earnest testament of its success in the future work it is to do."

Despite its promising beginnings and widespread support among influential white Georgians, the Black Mammy Memorial failed to develop into the great institution Harris envisioned. In fact, the institute quickly disappeared from the Athens scene, leaving only speculation concerning the reasons for its demise. The death of Booker T. Washington in 1915 and the rise of a new generation of leaders like W.E.B. Dubois, who demanded equal rights for blacks, probably eroded support for the school in the black community. Another reason could have been Harris's increasing involvement in Clarke County's public school system.

Following his tenure as principal of the West Broad School, Harris was appointed principal of the old Athens High and Industrial School in 1917. He vigorously resumed his efforts to incorporate industrial training into the public school curriculum. Domestic sciences were taught in a small two-room building on the school campus. The department was supplied with stoves and received $4 a month with which to buy foodstuffs. The high school also had a physics department with a small collection of apparatus for conducting experiments.

Under Harris's supervision, evening vocational classes were added to the curriculum at the high school. Adults were given the opportunity to learn cooking, sewing, home nursing, carpentry, masonry and the rudiments of bookkeeping. According to Willie Mae Mullins, "The rooms were filled with eager students." When plans had been drawn for the new high school to relieve overcrowding in the black system, Harris was instrumental in having it equipped with an elaborate manual training shop.

Harris's ideas regarding the importance of vocational and industrial education may have come of age in Clarke County by 1914. A revealing statement by the superintendent of Clarke County schools in the annual report that year documents the success of the industrial department at the black high school:

> I desire to say, as I have before, that I think this work is entirely too good to be given to the Negro exclusively. It seems to me that the next great move for us to make is to give the white boy a chance to educate his brains through his hand.

Five years after Harris's death, a writer for the Lavonia Times offered the following assessment of his contributions to the education of black Georgians: His most significant accomplishment "was to educate his friends at the University—in the needs of Negro children and the needs of their teachers. That word spread through the University, and through the state; changing attitudes, giving new hope to Negroes, and new courage to public school officials." The writer concluded, "That was the great work of Samuel F. Harris."

The so-called Mammy Land, located in the eastern section of Athens, was eventually returned to the city government. On April 12, 1950, city officials deeded ten acres of the property to the Clarke County Board of Education for $1,000. East Athens Elementary School was constructed on a portion of the land a few years later. In the 1970s, the East Athens Community Center was constructed on another parcel, title to which had been transferred back to the city by the board of education. Today, the East Athens Neighborhood Health Center and other community-based organizations are located on the property.

Harris died of heart failure on July 1,1935. Two days later, hundreds of mourners from "all walks of life and all races" assembled at First A.M.E. Church in Athens to pay tribute to the well-known educator. In his memory, a national honor society chapter, a local branch of the Young Men's Christian Association, a high school and a middle school were named for him. During his sixty years of life, Samuel Harris rose from the depths of poverty to the highest level of prominence in the field of education.

Although he enjoyed opportunities far beyond the reach of other members of his race, Harris never lost sight of the fact that the great majority of his people were victimized by racism and oppression. His tireless advocacy raised the moral consciousness of white leaders to the plight of black students and teachers in Georgia's segregated public school systems. Professor Samuel F. Harris' legacy of support for public education serves as an important lesson for today and the future.

A 40TH ANNIVERSARY UPDATE

In 2006 four University of Georgia students, Timothy Evans, Jamel Harvey, Kellen Williams Singleton and Jamarl Glenn began a quest to immortalize Harris' educational legacy by securing his college degree from the university. After reading *A Story Untold,* the students were inspired to redress what they believed was gross miscarriage of justice: Harris was denied the college degree he earned because of his race. Following three years of intense research and investigation, the young men officially petitioned UGA's administration to award Harris an honorary or posthumous degree.

According to Dr. Mary Frances Early, UGA's first African-American graduate, awarding Harris a degree would be "a recognition of Professor Harris' accomplishments at UGA and beyond, and it would also affirm the University of Georgia's willingness to reach beyond normal policies." She added, "Harris couldn't receive a degree because of segregation. There's no reason that he shouldn't be granted a degree, now that the university is desegregated and is recognizing other pioneers of color."

Granting an honorary or posthumous degree by the university would honor Professor Samuel F. Harris' genius, tenacity and commitment to education. It would also acknowledge the courage of the white UGA professors who violated strict cultural and legal sanctions to assist young Sam Harris in his pursuit of educational excellence.

Dr. Ida Mae Johnson Hiram

MEDICAL PIONEERS

Men and Women Who Healed and Helped

Ignored, distorted, deliberately concealed
or innocently omitted,
the fact remains that by and large
most of the information about the Negro in medicine
remains unknown in the history of the United States.

JOHN L.S. HOLLOMAN, JR.
President, National Medical Association

At the turn of the twentieth century, one of the most distinguished doctors in Athens was Dr. Blanche Thompson, a black woman. Born in Greensboro, Georgia in 1880, she was educated in the public schools of Atlanta, Atlanta University, and Walden University in Nashville before entering Nashville's Meharry Medical College in 1897.

Four years later, she earned her medical degree and was qualified to practice in both Alabama and Georgia. She developed a large practice "not only among the colored people, but also [among] a number of Athens's best white citizens." She had "the distinction of introducing the first surgery done in Athens by all Negro physicians..." But Dr. Thompson's crowning achievement was the development of plans which eventually resulted in the establishment of a sanitorium for the treatment of tuberculosis.

In 1978, Dr. Donarell R. Green, a veteran of over thirty years of medical practice, was the only remaining member of a group of approximately twenty black doctors and dentists (including two women) who practiced in and around Athens during the first half of the twentieth century. The most fundamental, most important characteristic they had in common was a commitment to upgrading medical care for blacks and poor people in Northeast Georgia.

Dr. Green shared this commitment. In 1947, he helped found the Northeast Georgia Medical Association, an organization of black doctors in northeast Georgia who pledged themselves to the improvement of their profession as well as their own medical abilities. Dr. Green served on the medical staff of the Athens Neighborhood Health Center, which provides quality health care for all area residents, with fees based on the patient's ability to pay, as well as on the staff of St. Mary's Hospital and Athens Regional Hospital.

Dr. Blanche B.S. Thompson

Like all except two of his medical predecessors, Dr. Green graduated from Meharry Medical College in Nashville. And like most of the other black medical pioneers, Dr. Green was born into a medical family. His father was an Atlanta physician, the son of a midwife. Dr. Green's mother was a school principal.

Born in Atlanta on December 22, 1908, Dr. Green attended that city's public schools. He subsequently received his undergraduate degree from Talladega College in Talladega, Alabama in 1933. While there, he met his future wife, Kathleen Williams, a native of Long Island, New York. They were married two years after Green's graduation.

In March of 1946, after earning his doctor of medicine degree at Meharry and serving as a physician in the U.S. Army, Dr. Green settled in Athens. He opened a medical office in the Morton Building on Washington Street where he maintained a private practice, as did all the other early black doctors and dentists.

In 1953, Dr. Green purchased the Susan Medical Center, a small maternity hospital on the corner of Hancock Avenue and Chase Street, and operated it until 1964. It had been founded in 1946 by Dr. Andrew Jones, who named it after his mother. Dr. Jones built the hospital with donations from local blacks and whites, and from Athenian Clubs in large northern metropolitan areas.

The most prominent of Athens's earlier black physicians was Dr. William H. Harris, who was also the principal organizer and largest stockholder in the E. D. Harris Drug Company, the first black-owned drugstore in Athens. (Dr. Blanche Thompson, the first black woman to practice medicine in Athens, was another stockholder in the Harris Drug Company.)

Harris received a silver cup from prominent black citizens in appreciation of twenty years of service as "citizen and physician." This presentation was made on March 3, 1913, to officially recognize Harris's outstanding medical and civic contributions to the black community in Athens.

Twenty years earlier, for example, Dr. Harris had cofounded the Georgia State Medical Association in Augusta. He served as the association's third vice president and as chairman of the Committee on Constitution and Bylaws. He was elected vice president of the association in 1910, and was elected president of the medical section a year later.

Throughout his long career, Dr. Harris continued to study medicine in order to improve his skills and keep up to date. He was valedictorian of his graduating class at Meharry Medical College in Nashville in 1893. After practicing for a few years in his new office on Clayton Street in Athens, Harris decided to take a course in surgery at the Harvard Post-Graduate Medical School. He later continued his advanced surgical training at the New York School of Clinical Medicine in Bellevue Hospital and at the Massachusetts General Hospital in Boston.

In addition to his medical studies and practice, Dr. Harris was an important figure in the national Republican party. At the twentieth national Republican convention in 1932, Harris was asked to serve on the committee whose members officially informed President Herbert Hoover of his nomination for the presidency.

He was also committed to bettering the lot of his fellow man. In 1897, Dr. Harris founded the Improved Order of Samaritans in Athens—a fraternal insurance organization originally established to provide indigent blacks financial help with funeral expenses.

Among Athens's black dental pioneers was a husband and wife team, Ida Mae and Lace Hiram. In June 1901, Ida Mae Johnson, a nineteen-year-old Athens native, married Lace C. Hiram, one of Athens's first black dentists. Encouraged by her husband to continue her education, Ida Hiram graduated from Knox Institute in 1905, and received her doctor of dentistry degree from Meharry Medical College five years later.

Dr. Hiram had the distinction of being the first black woman dentist in Athens, and the first black woman to pass the Georgia Dental Board exams. She practiced dentistry in Athens for fifty-five years until she was eighty-three-years-old.

Dr. Vernon Wimberly and Dr. Andrew Jones

Four years after Dr. Hiram opened her practice in Athens, Dr. Isadore Horace Burney was also practicing dentistry here, and in several other northeast Georgia cities as well. Dr. Burney established and operated dental offices in Madison, Elberton, and Union Point.

Like the other black medical and dental pioneers, Dr. Burney worked continuously to improve the health and sanitary conditions of black people in and around Athens. He also lectured frequently to various institutions, schools, and societies.

Some of Athens's black physicians and dentists had two professions. The most notable of these was Dr. Charles S. Haynes. Both minister and physician, Dr. Haynes tended to the spiritual and physical ills of local blacks for many years.

At the age of twenty-eight, Haynes was ordained a minister of the Colored Congregationalist Church. Only one year later, he graduated with honors from the Leonard Medical School in Raleigh, North Carolina. Born in New Amsterdam in British Guiana, he was educated in local schools and in the London missionary schools.

After his graduation from medical school, Dr. Haynes was sent to Athens by the American Missionary Association to serve as pastor of the Colored Congregationalist Church on the corner of Pope and Meigs streets. During his twenty years in that pulpit, he worked tirelessly among prisoners and the poor. He increased the church's membership, but also had time to work in the community to improve the health of Athens citizens. One of his most successful projects was the founding of a Department of Nursing at Athens High and Industrial School in 1918.

The unique Jackson family probably made the most out-standing contribution to the health and welfare of Athenians. There were five brothers in the family: Farris, Albon, Thomas, Samuel, and Burnett. Three were medical doctors, while the other two were dentists.

Other black physicians, such as Dr. F. Earl McLendon, practiced in Athens for a short period of time and then migrated to larger metropolitan areas. During the early 1940s, McLendon moved to Atlanta where he established a large, lucrative medical practice. In 1946, he founded McLendon Hospital. Located in southwest Atlanta, the facility was originally equipped with sixty beds and, according to one researcher, was "clean and nicely furnished."

The blacks who were practicing medicine in the Atlanta area during that period were generally pleased with the operation and maintenance of the hospital. Their major criticism was that McLendon Hospital did not provide training facilities for medical interns.

But some white observers were much more critical of McLendon Hospital. One person referred to it and another black Atlanta hospital as "nothing but butcher shops." He also stated that "the 'nigger' doctors cut a person out at these hospitals, then send him down to Grady where he dies." As this statement suggests, opinions of the professional practices of black doctors and dentists, as well as of the quality of care that their patients received, were sometimes colored by deep-seated racial prejudice.

In the South and to a lesser degree in the northern states, qualified black students were denied admission to white medical schools until the early 1960s. In 1900 there were seven black medical schools scattered throughout the United States, but with the exception of Meharry Medical College and Howard University, the schools were generally ill-equipped and understaffed.

During that same year, Abraham Flexner published a controversial report concerning the condition of medical education in America. Entitled Medical Education in the United States, the "report strongly influenced the setting of standards for medical colleges and led to the closing of all Negro medical colleges with the exception of Howard and Meharry."

For many black physicians in the South, policies denying them admission to local American Medical Association affiliates created severe economic and professional problems.

Dr. W.H. Harris

E.D. Harris Drug Store

> Non-membership meant denial of hospital affiliation since doctors, as a matter of course, had to be accredited by their county societies before they could be eligible for hospital appointments.
>
> To Negro doctors in the South, such exclusion meant professional stagnation and economic deprivation. Without hospital connections, they were denied the opportunity of pursuing their medical education and training. Any hope they might entertain of doing research had to be abandoned.

Hospitals and clinics also enforced "whites-only" policies, even in the case of medical emergencies. One shocking example involved a native Athenian. In November of 1931, Julliette Derricotte, an internationally known organizer for the Young Women's Christian Association, was enroute from Fisk University in Tennessee to Athens when the car in which she was riding collided with another vehicle near Dalton, Georgia.

She and another passenger were critically injured, but because of their color they were not admitted to the white hospital in Dalton. Instead, they were transported over rough roads to Chattanooga, Tennessee. Her companion died enroute, and Julliette Derricotte died a few hours later.

Although no incident of this nature was ever recorded in Athens, the local clinic, as well as St. Mary's and Athens General hospitals, maintained racially segregated facilities. In 1945, sixty-eight beds at Athens General were reserved for whites and twenty-two were designated for black patients. Single and double occupancy rooms were provided for both races, as well as ward space.

Facilities for blacks at privately owned St. Mary's Hospital were more limited. Out of a total of sixty-eight beds, only fourteen could be used by blacks. Twenty-four private rooms, three double occupancy rooms, and three wards were available to whites, but black patients were treated only in the wards.

Mrs. Agnes Wingfield can still recall the pain and sorrow of having to visit her physician husband, the late Dr. Charles Wingfield, in the segregated ward of Athens General. At that time the "colored ward" was located in the basement of the hospital. But even this was an improvement over the four-room building in the backyard of Athens General which was reserved for black patients prior to the 1940s. As Mrs. Virginia Edwards described it, the structure "resembled a chicken coop that was divided into two rooms—one for men and one for women—with two beds in each room."

But despite the Jim Crow policies of the medical facilities, black Athenians were, relatively speaking, better off than thousands of other black Georgians who lived in areas where even segregated medical facilities were unavailable.

In the 1960s, discriminatory medical and hospital policies became a prime target of civil rights activists throughout the nation. In March 1966, at the second national convention of the Medical Committee for Human Rights in Chicago, Dr. Martin Luther King, Jr. told the delegates, "Of all the forms of inequality, injustice in health is the most shocking and the most inhuman..."

Dr. Isadore Horace Burney

The backbone of discriminatory policies in many federally subsidized hospitals in America was an amendment to the Hill-Burton Act—an act which authorized "matching Federal grants, ranging from one-third to two-thirds of the total cost of construction and equipment, to public and non-profit private health facilities." The amendment allowed segregated health facilities "for separate population groups if the facilities and services were of like quality for each group."

During the seventeen-year period that followed the approval of the Hill-Burton Act, nearly all of the 7,000 medical facilities built under the provisions of the act were of this so-called nondiscriminatory type. As interpreted by the general counsel of the U.S. Department of Health, Education and Welfare, this meant that:

1. No person could be denied admission as a patient because of race, creed, or color to that portion of the facility constructed with federal funds. However, he could be denied admission to other portions of the facility.
2. No patient could be denied any service essential to his medical care.
3. Patients could be segregated within the facility by race, creed, or color.
4. Professionally qualified persons could be denied staff privileges, and interns and residents could be denied training on account of race, creed, or color.

In 1963, the movement to establish equal access to health facilities was advanced by a federal court decision in the case of *Simkins v. Cone.* On appeal, the Fourth Circuit Court reversed a lower court decision and ruled that two Wilmington, North Carolina, hospitals could not deny professional medical training or staff positions to persons solely on the basis of race. The Court also ruled that the separate-but-equal provision of the Hill-Burton Act was unconstitutional under the Fifth and Fourteenth Amendments.

The U.S. Supreme Court refused to review the Simkins decision and thus upheld it. Finally, in March 1964, the Department of Health, Education and Welfare announced Title VI of the 1964 Civil Rights Act which forbade any type of discrimination based on race, color, creed or national origin in hospitals built with Hill-Burton funds. This requirement was later expanded to include all medical facilities receiving any type of federal aid.

In 1978, medical care was available to everyone regardless of color. However, there were only two black practitioners: Dr. Matthew McRae, Jr., who established his dental practice in Athens in 1975, and Dr. Donarell Green. Dr. Green died in 1980, after practicing medicine in the Classic City for nearly thirty-five years, and is revered today for his unselfish and untiring medical services to the Athens Community.

When Dr. Green first came to Athens, recalled Sampson Edwards,

> He rolled up his sleeves and went to work healing the sick, giving advice when he was asked, never denying anyone service when he was needed, whether they had the money to pay him or not.... When we called on him, be it 2, 3, 4, or 5 o'clock in the morning, he would be there in a jiffy.

After Dr. Green's death, the Susan Building at 1127 W. Hancock was leased and renovated by Michael Thurmond and Janice Mathis, who practiced law there with various partners until 2000, when it returned to the Green family. Today is it the law office of Donarell Green IV and Fredrell Green, grandsons of Dr. Donarell Green.

Today, the professional medical community has grown to once again number some twenty practitioners. Dr. McRae has expanded his comprehensive dental practice with the addition of Drs. Wolanda P. Hardy and Darlene Perez, and Dr. Claude T. DuBose's has established a dental practice in East Athens.

Dr. Donnarell Green

The Susan Medical Center

Dr. Wayne Morris, who served as physician to the Neighborhood Health Center before opening a private practice in 1980, is the longest practicing local African-American medical doctor. Other medical practitioners include Dr. Zaewea Adeduntan, Dr. Beze Adogu, Dr. Martine Adogu, Dr. Gena Alexander-Albert, Dr. James Brown, Dr. Diane Dunston, Dr. Anthony Gordon, Dr. Peter Johnson, Dr. Debra Jordan, Dr. Leah D. Lowman, Dr. Victor E. Payton, Dr. Patricia Pelham-Harris, and Dr. Eric Wilson.

A 40TH ANNIVERSARY UPDATE

Dr. Matthew McRae Jr.

Dr. Matthew McRae Jr. opened his first dental practice in 1973 and has served the Athens community as a leading dentist for more than 45 years. Since then, Dr. McRae has grown his practice, McRae Family Dentistry, from a 740 square foot facility to more than 5,000 square feet. Like his predecessors, he believes strongly in not setting limits and the importance of giving back. The McRae Family Dentistry practice regularly volunteers at various community health clinics and provide free dental care. Dr. McRae also co-founded the MCG's McRae-Orrington Dental Scholarship fund and established the Athens Humans Relations Annual Scholarship to encourage more black students to practice dentistry. A native of Helena, Georgia, Dr. McRae graduated from Fort Valley State

College, the Medical College of Georgia Dentistry and received a Mastership with the Academy of General Dentistry in 1993.

Dr. Claude T. DuBose

Dr. Claude T. DuBose opened his practice, East Athens Family Dentistry, more than 30 years ago. Noted for providing quality care, Dr. DuBose was listed as one of the best dentists in Athens, Georgia by Opencare.com. A native of Elberton, Georgia, Dr. DuBose graduated from Elbert County Comprehensive High School, Clark College in Atlanta, Meharry Medical College School of Dentistry and completed a hospital Dentistry certification in 1987. In 2007, Dr. DuBose was the recipient of the 2007 Elbertonian Award for outstanding community service from the Elbert County NAACP.

Dr. Farris T. Johnson Jr.

Dr. Farris T. Johnson Jr. is a native Athenian and has practiced medicine in Athens since 1985. Dr. Johnson's medical experience includes practicing as an emergency medicine physician and eight years in the United States Air Force as a family physician and flight surgeon. Before opening his own practice, Johnson and Murthy Family Practice, Dr. Johnson served the residents of Athens as a physician at the Athens Area Commencement Center, Athens Nurses Clinic, Athens Regional Physician Services, Athens Regional Medical Center and St. Mary's Hospital. Dr. Johnson is board-certified by the American Board of Family Practice and also serves as an assistant professor in the Essentials of Clinical Medicine course at the Georgia Regents University/ University of Georgia Medical Partnership. Dr. Johnson attended public school in

Clarke County and graduated from Burney-Harris High School. He attended Morehouse College and received his medical education from the University of Pittsburgh School of Medicine in 1977, and completed his internship in 1978 and his residency in 1980, both at Malcolm Grow Medical Center at Andrews Air Force Base, Maryland. Dr. Johnson is the son of two long-time Clarke County educators, the late Farris Johnson, Sr. and the late Mable Johnson.

The Athens Neighborhood Health Center (ANHC) Inc., is a not-for-profit medical facility born out of President Lyndon B. Johnson's Model for Cities Initiative. The initiative was created to reduce poverty and support local municipalities in addressing social issues that plagued the poor. Three community activists, Jesse Barrett, Miriam Moore, and Evelyn C. Neely, worked with the Athens City Council and local leaders to secure a multi-million dollar federal grant designated for 35 projects including establishing a clinic to serve Athens citizens. In 1971, the ANHC started out as a trailer. In the mid-1980s, a fire destroyed the trailer and the clinic relocated to the central office's current location, 675 College Avenue. The center expanded in 2000 and opened a second location in East Athens. Today, the ANHC consists of three facilities including a pharmacy and has provided affordable health care to Athens' medically underserved for nearly 50 years.

Dr. Diane Dunston

In 1987, Dr. Diane Dunston began her medical career as a pediatrician at the Athens Neighborhood Health Center (ANHC) and partnered with Dr. Gail Hurley in serving Athens' poorest communities. Founded by three community activists, ANHC was the first community clinic in Athens to provide medical services to the working poor, the homeless and the uninsured. Dr. Dunston was instrumental in increasing the center's impact on decreasing health disparities and successfully led the effort to regain the center's Federally Qualified Community Health Center designation. Dr. Dunston also led ANHC's expansion efforts which included adding a pharmacy to ensure patients receive affordable medications. A native of Washington D.C., Dr. Dunston completed her medical training at the George Washington University School of Medicine and a residency at the Children's National Medical Center. Dr. Dunston dedicated 30 years to treating Athenians who desperately needed care and retired from the ANHC as the Chief Medical Officer in 2017.

Dr. Gail Hurley

Dr. Gail Hurley is a native Athenian and deeply rooted in the Athens community. Dr. Hurley began her career in Athens through the National Health Services Corps, a federal program designed to assist communities in recruiting and retaining physicians. As a new doctor, she practiced at several community health clinics and devoted much of her time to healing and treating patients who needed medical attention the most. In 1987, she came to work at the Athens Neighborhood Health Center and has served as a general practitioner providing quality care for more than 30 years. Dr. Hurley attended the segregated public school systems of Athens, Georgia and was one of the few African-Americans to enroll at Athens High School. After completing high school, she graduated from Howard University, the Medical College of Georgia and the University Hospital in Augusta, Georgia and was one of a handful of African-Americans to receive a Doctorate of Medicine in 1976.

Lucius Henry Holsey

LUCIUS HENRY HOLSEY

The Slave Who Founded a College

I had to walk the town
to get up pupils for the school [Paine College],
Such was the condition and feeling against the school
that I had to pay the students fifty cents a day to attend.
... had it not been for this strategy and cunning,
there could not have been started Paine College in that city.
Not a man who belonged to our church would help,
but derided the movement, hissed it, and howled it to the ground.

LUCIUS HENRY HOLSEY

During his seventy-eight years of life, Lucius Henry Holsey rose from the depths of illiteracy and slavery to the highest levels of prominence in religion and education. When he first arrived in Athens in the winter of 1857, he was fourteen years old, the product of racially mixed parents, and "the property of Col. R. M. Johnston, a professor at the state college."

Holsey and his biographer, John Brother Cade, point to his years of residence as a slave in Athens as one of the most important periods of his life. (Cade, the biographer, was himself a 1914 graduate of Knox Institute in Athens, and a 1915 graduate of the printing department of the same institution. He served for many years as the chief registrar at Paine College in Augusta.)

The little college town and its institution of higher learning served as the primal catalytic agents in the creation of Holsey's desire to learn and his conversion to the Christian faith.

The atmosphere of the city and the college created in Holsey what he later described as "an insatiable craving for some knowledge of books." Although it was against the law for slaves to read and write, Holsey was prepared to take whatever risks might be necessary in order to learn.

His first task was to obtain money for the books he needed. Holsey wrote,

> I gathered and sold all the rags that I could, and sold them that I might get some money with which to buy books. After weeks of toil and intense vigilance in gathering and watching for rags that belonged to the first man that laid hands upon them, I had accumulated about thirty pounds. These I stuffed into the legs and seat of a pair of old white pantaloons,

> the cast-off garment of a large and long-legged man. At night after tea, I was allowed to "go downtown" for recreation. I hired a boy to help me carry the rags to sell them to the rag merchant... The rags were sold and the money was mine.

With the money, Holsey bought the books which he thought belonged in his basic library: "two Webster blue back spellers, a common school dictionary, Milton's *Paradise Lost*, and a Bible." Then, with the help of "white children and an old colored man," Holsey began his lifelong task of self-education.

He studied at night by the flickering light of the fireplace, or snatched moments here and there during the day in order to learn to read and write. In his autobiography, Holsey explains his surreptitious method of learning

> Day by day, I took a leaf from one of the spelling books, and so folded it that one or two of the lessons were on the outside as if printed on a card. This I put in the pocket of my vest or coat, and when I was sitting on the carriage, walking the yard or streets, or in the dining room, I would take out my spelling leaf. catch a word and commit it to memory.

At the age of fifteen, a significant event occurred in Holsey's life: he was converted by Henry McNeal Turner, and became a member of the Methodist church in Athens. Preacher Turner, who later became a prominent bishop of the A.M.E. Church, a politician, and a proponent of black nationalism, attracted huge audiences of whites and blacks throughout the Southeast as a traveling evangelist for the white Methodist Episcopal Church, South. When Turner came to Athens, Holsey recalled, he "preached every night to appreciative congregations, and under his powerful sermons I experienced a change of heart, and became a zealous member of the church."

For the rest of his life, as Holsey himself wrote, his history was "the history of the church of which I am a member. Its history cannot be written nor its records compiled without me as one of the chief actors in its drama..." In 1861, when Holsey was nineteen, the war that divided America and ultimately freed the slaves began, prompting Col. Johnston to move his family and his slave to Hancock County until the end of the war. After his emancipation, Holsey realized one of his greatest ambitions by becoming a licensed preacher for the Methodist Episcopal Church, South, in 1868. He was appointed "senior preacher" in the Hancock Circuit, which covered the entire county and included seven black churches.

Unfortunately, Holsey's voice was weak. As for the all-important "dramatics of preaching, he then had none." People went to sleep during his sermons. They longed for the junior preacher, a Reverend E. B. Oliver, who possessed "a clear, loud, high, ringing voice [of] rare depths of pathos and sweetness"—the kind of voice which inspired congregations.

> One of the most difficult things with which I had to contend was to get from under the withering blight of his [Oliver's] trumpet voice... I could not move the multitudes to tears like the junior preacher, although it was understood by the people that I was "the deeper reasoner," as they used to say, but was "no preacher."

Holsey was determined to overcome his problem. He asked himself:

> What shall I do to make it [his voice] thunder, scream, screech, howl, or roar as did the junior preacher? I often spent an hour in the woods, and from a pine stump, serving as a temporary pulpit, I would take the text to be used on the next Sabbath, and from it preach in a loud voice... This practice helped me wonderfully, and soon I began to thunder and rattle like the other big preachers.

In December 1870, in Jackson, Tenn., Holsey took part in the organizing conference of the Colored Methodist Episcopal Church in America, a separate organization of the black members of the Methodist Episcopal

Church, South. Holsey was also responsible for compiling a hymnal and a manual of discipline for the denomination, which had 12,998 members and 61 preachers.

In 1873, five years after he was licensed to preach, Holsey became—at age thirty— "one of the youngest men ever elected bishop in any age or church." He was elected and consecrated in an extraordinary session at Trinity Church, Augusta.

In 1881, the thirty-eight-year-old bishop was awarded one of Methodism's highest honors. While attending an Ecumenical Council meeting in London, Holsey "preached in City Road Chapel, the distinguished Mother of Methodism, from the same little box pulpit from which John Wesley preached the gospel of free grace."

But the establishment of Paine Institute in Augusta was Holsey's foremost accomplishment in education. The thirty-nine-year-old Holsey went before the bishops at the General Conference of the Methodist Episcopal Church, South and presented an urgent plea for the establishment of a college for the express purpose of educating black preachers and teachers. He felt this was the job of the church, since the state provided primary instruction for black children.

The institute was incorporated a year later in 1883, and later renamed Paine College. It remains, almost one hundred years later, as a monument to Holsey and the many people, both black and white, who contributed to its growth.

In 1897, the Colored Methodist Episcopal Church appointed Bishop Holsey to go on a nationwide speaking tour to raise funds for the erection of "a suitable school building" on the Paine College campus. The black and white audiences he spoke to saw before them a slender, tall, handsome man in the traditional dark suit and clerical collar. He had fair skin, a lofty forehead framed by auburn hair, and looked out at them with "clear and penetrating" brown eyes.

At first, Holsey was disheartened by the lukewarm reception he received in surrounding states. But his luck turned when he returned to the

Classic City he had left as a slave. As bishop of the Colored Methodist Episcopal Church, he was summoned to address the North Georgia Conference and had, as his biographer puts it, "his most single success in the matter of collecting money for the Paine Institute."

The *New York Independent* gave the following account of Holsey's presentation to Athens citizens in December of 1897:

> The call was for $1,000 at least, and $1,526 was raised... Is it not something that such a man as Holsey is the product of Southern Civilization and Southern Methodism? — The Negro, said he, is here to stay; he has been, and is now, a strong factor in the civilization of this country.

Holsey himself was encouraged by the generous response of his home town. He wrote, "This collection ... was a record smasher and is the highest collection made by our church. It was simply phenomenal..." In an article for the Gospel Trumpet, he concluded, "Everywhere among the Southern Methodist people, there is a new awakening and a sincere desire to help the Afro-Americans to rise from the darkness of the past."

Two years after this record-smashing collection, Haygood Memorial Hall, "a substantial four story" brick structure, was occupied on the Paine campus. The building was an Augusta landmark for about seventy years until it was destroyed by fire in the summer of 1968. It has since been replaced by a new multi-million dollar structure christened Haygood-Holsey Hall. Ironically, Holsey Hall—named in honor of Paine's founder and formerly the oldest building on the school's campus—had to be razed in order to make room for the new structure.

A firm believer in education for blacks, Holsey also had a hand in establishing three other schools: Lane College in Jackson, Tennessee; Helen B. Cobb Institute in Barnesville, Georgia; and Holsey Industrial Institute in Cordele, Georgia.

Haygood Memorial Hall at Paine College

Although Holsey was the principal organizer of Paine College, an institution that has served as a model for racial co-operation in the South for nearly a century, he was a separatist throughout his adult life. He believed the only salvation for the black man in America was his complete physical separation from the white race.

As early as 1866, when he was only twenty-three years old, he was advocating the migration of "Afro-Americans" as he called the black people, from among white Americans, particularly in the South. He also realized that some southern whites would be more willing to contribute funds to educational institutions which were preparing their graduates to return to Africa.

He stated the basis of his beliefs in an article in the *Atlanta Constitution* in 1899.

> Each year the racial differences are rendering it more and more impossible for the whites and blacks to occupy the same territory, and there is nothing for the black man to do but to move or remain here as an oppressed and degraded race.

"America is not the final place, not even a good place for the Negro," Holsey said at an Emancipation Proclamation Day celebration at Sparta in 1866. He prophesied that Africa would someday command a position of prominence in world affairs and that, because of the efforts of some "great and good men, this country is fitting the Negro for his fatherland in Africa...."

In fact, as his biographer writes:

> He predicted a future where the dark continent will be equal to any other. In vision he saw the busy world of Africa engaged in mining and manufacturing...and that if the Afro-American continues to increase in civilization, he will return to Africa and claim it for Christ.

Many whites readily accepted the idea of black emigration to Africa because it was, to them, an easy and sure answer to the problems of integration. Besides, Holsey defended his philosophy against its detractors by pointing out that Thomas Jefferson, Abraham Lincoln, Daniel Webster, and Athens native Henry Grady had previously expressed similar beliefs.

But by 1898, Bishop Holsey realized that the exodus to Africa was a remote possibility at best. He therefore began to advocate a compromise plan: the creation of a black nation somewhere in the United States, "possibly in Oklahoma or New Mexico." It is "impossible for the two separate and distinct races to live together in the same territory in harmonious relationship," Holsey said in a speech before a church congregation in Washington, D.C. Because of the "infinite volume of racial prejudices," he called on the federal government to set aside "some territory or parts of the public domain for the specific purpose of forming a state or states for qualified Negro American citizens."

His separatist beliefs antagonized those, black and white, who believed that America was the rightful home of the black man and that black and white could live side by side. John Cade suggests, then refutes, the contention that Holsey's philosophy caused a rift between himself and the white administration at Paine College. But Holsey maintained his beliefs until he died at the age of seventy-eight. "The Union of States will never be fully and perfectly recemented . . . until black Ham and white Japheth dwell together in separate tents," he wrote toward the end of his life.

He states his belief again in this excerpt from his unpublished autobiography:

> More than fifty years ago I . . . asked for a state or states in the union of states for the colored race. Ever since that time I have not only marked the trend of events but I have never dropped the thought out of my mind for a day . . . and I have seen nothing in the evolution of the decades to change my views then expressed.
>
> Fifty-four years have passed away since freedom was declared to the four million slaves ... [they have] all the versatile and dominant elements to respond to the greatest demands and the highest calls. This being the case, the colored race will never be satisfied or rest in peace until it is allowed the same rights of full citizenship that other races enjoy.
>
> Hence, the conflict will continue and racial antagonisms and bitterness will grow larger, deeper, and broader, until the whole hemisphere

> of the civic state will be filled with conflicting and contending forces; and the black man will be the extreme sufferer.

Holsey remained physically active throughout his long, productive life even though he suffered from consumption. As a young cleric, he usually walked to other cities and towns, with the aid of his ever-present cane, when his religious duties required him to travel. Even in his later years he often disdained the luxury of horse-powered transportation.

At his death in 1920, the following eulogy was published in *The Christian Index*:

> He could make smart men go back to their books and fools take to the woods. He could lay any man on his dissecting table and hold him up piece by piece... He cared not much for chasing rabbits; he liked the trail of deer or bear or even lions.

Paine College President Dr. Julius Scott made the following observation:

> It was Bishop Holsey's vision and commitment to higher learning that served as the genesis for the creation of this institution. He was without any doubt the person most singly responsible for the creation of Paine College.

The chaplain of Paine College, Dr. Maurice Cherry, called him "a person of great vision and... far ahead of his times. He was perceptive, analytical and hard-working." But perhaps the most poignant epitaph was written by Bishop Holsey himself when he said:

> From youth until the present, life has been an unremitting struggle and a perpetual series of trials and conflicts. I have helped every man, woman, and child that I could, and have tried to bear the burdens of others as the scriptures direct.

Hall Johnson

HALL JOHNSON

World Famous Conductor, Arranger, Composer

The Green Pastures ... has meant many things
to many Negro observers.
... for myself—I feel... [it is]
the finest dramatic expression, so far,
of the spirit that imbues the Negro Spirituals,
and that that spirit of proud humility,
of unswerving determination,
of unalterable love,
is the finest that could possibly sway
the destinities of any people—bond or free.

HALL JOHNSON

There's a plaque in athens city hall designating the Classic City as a "Landmark of American Music," and proclaiming a native Athenian one of "America's Most Distinguished Black Musicians." He was Hall Johnson, grandson of slaves, who became a composer, arranger, and choir director of national and international acclaim.

The son of the Reverend William Decker Johnson, young Hall was born in the midst of a late winter snowstorm on March 12, 1888. He learned spirituals from his grandmother, a former slave, who sang to him by the hour while he listened and copied down the words. Later, when he learned to write music, he also wrote down the melodies.

While music was always part of his life, Johnson did not begin to study it seriously until he entered college. His first music lessons were taught by James Davis, a well-known Athenian who was music instructor at the Baxter Street School and was also a city mail carrier for many years.

When he was fifteen, Johnson graduated from Knox Institute in Athens and attended Atlanta University for one year. But he transferred to Allen University in Columbia, South Carolina when his father was appointed president of the school. While there, he taught himself to play a violin his mother had given him, using a "ten-cent instructor." A short time later, he was proficient enough to play with a dance orchestra in a local summer resort.

In 1908, college degree in hand, the twenty-year-old Johnson set off for Philadelphia where he worked and studied music at the University of Pennsylvania's School of Music. In addition, he took violin lessons at the Hahn School of Music, and was a regular patron of the Philadelphia Orchestra's weekly concerts. In 1910, he graduated from the university and was awarded the Simon Haessler Prize for the best composition for orchestra and chorus.

When World War I broke out, Johnson took his music to the battlefield. He was a member of the Jim Europe Band, the official band of New York's 369th Colored Infantry. One of the few black fighting units of that period, the 369th regiment was also one of the best. The French government awarded every member of the regiment the *Croix de Guerre* for gallantry.

After the war, Johnson and several friends formed the original Hall Johnson Negro Choir in Harlem. The group grew rapidly under the leadership of its thirty-seven-year-old director. At one time it had some three hundred members, although Johnson chose only the best fifty voices for most of the choir's concert tours.

The choir's first concert was in the Pythian Temple, an auditorium in New York City, three years after the group was founded. Johnson explained his method of presenting the music in an introduction to his concert. He said he wanted the traditional folk melodies to be "given in a manner which will reproduce the fervor of the camp meeting which gave them birth." He continued:

> Beyond clarity of diction and fair precision of attack, no attempt is made to secure a perfect choral ensemble... We believe this enables us to preserve an emotional content that would be lost with greater refinement.

A month later, on March 20,1928, the choir gave its second concert in New York's prestigious Town Hall—a sure sign that the group had made it. Other engagements followed quickly. In August the choir appeared jointly with the New York Philharmonic Symphony Orchestra in New York City's Lewisohn Stadium for the first of six consecutive annual concerts with the Philharmonic. In fact, the gradually expanding choir was kept busy with appearances in New York and on tour for the next eight years.

Their programs consisted mostly of authentic black music, both religious and secular. Among them were spirituals—"devotional songs, episodic songs, or songs of religious experience"— as well as lullabies, social songs, songs about animals, and work songs—"songs of the levee, the rock pile, and the cotton field."

The skillful simplicity and earthiness of Johnson's arrangements produced rave reviews from many northeastern critics. Conductor Willem van Hoogstraten observed that the Johnson choir sang "as Negroes do when they do it spontaneously," because Johnson's arrangements avoided unnecessary sophistication. "They sing with the inexorable beat often lost by white singers," W.J. Henderson of the New York Sun wrote, adding that the choir used "the true Negro portamento suspected as the origin of jazz."

Audiences saw Johnson "lead the choir by [a] sign language of hands, arms, body, and head . . . that bore no conceivable relation to the ... white man's art of conducting," according to one reviewer. Tall and bespectacled, Johnson had "the longest imaginable arms" and the "supplest imaginable fingers," to quote one newspaper reporter.

After 1935, Hall Johnson spent most of his time on the West Coast, including Hollywood where he helped orchestrate a number of movies. One of his outstanding musical accomplishments was arranging, conducting, and composing some of the music for *The Green Pastures* which was both a play and a movie.

Written by Marc Connelly, the play was first presented at New York City's Mansfield Theatre on November 16,1930. The Green Pastures revealed the lighter side of the black religious experience by retelling eighteen episodes from the Bible in the dialect and psychology of southern blacks. In the play, heaven was represented as a gigantic fish fry, while "de Lawd" assumed the form of an immensely wise and charitable old black preacher who walked the earth and intermingled with his "chillun."

Johnson arranged twenty-three of the spirituals sung in the drama and composed two others. They included several familiar spirituals ranging in tempo from the mournful "Go Down Moses" to the exuberant "When the Saints Go Marchin' In."

Johnson also helped orchestrate *Swanee River, Way Down South, Cabin in the Sky*, and *Lost Horizon*, as well as other lesser known films.

Meanwhile his Hall Johnson Choir performed in movies, concerts, theater, radio, and television. Although it continued to make appearances on Broadway and other parts of the country, Johnson's work with films confined the choir mainly to concerts on the West Coast. In 1941, Johnson established the Festival Negro Choir of Los Angeles—a training group made up of two hundred voices. All the proceeds from their appearances were donated to a scholarship fund for talented needy black students.

The Hall Johnson Choir in the mid-1950s

Meanwhile, Johnson wrote a cantata, "Son of Man," and a play which evoked much controversy among critics throughout the country. Entitled *Run Li'l Chillun*, this music drama, which many people described as folk art, received mixed reviews. It was about the struggle between "an itinerant moon-worshiping group, the New Day Pilgrims," and a Negro Baptist church over the soul of the Baptist minister's son who had been seduced by a disciple of the nature cult. The two most controversial scenes were the ones depicting the Pilgrims' religious orgy in the woods and the Baptists' revival meeting.

Margaret Marshall of *The Nation* did not consider the play folk art.

"Far from being such," she wrote, "it showed that the author had very confused ideas himself of what he was up to." But Robert Garland of The New York Sun wrote that *Run Li'l Chillun* was "noble and magnificent, superb and appealing, frenzied and moving, elemental and emotional...."

After their West Coast stint, the Hall Johnson Choir toured France, Germany, and Austria on a goodwill mission for the United States government. And in 1951, the choir sang at the International Festival of Fine Arts in Berlin, under the baton of the sixty-three-year-old Johnson.

By now, Johnson's success as a composer, arranger, and director of the Hall Johnson Choir had brought him national and international acclaim. He continued making music and garnering more honors until the end of his long, productive life in 1971 at the age of eighty-three.

On Johnson's eighty-second birthday in 1970, Mayor John V. Lindsay of New York City presented him one of the city's most distinguished honors, the George Frederick Handel Award, for his unusual contributions to the world of music.

Shortly before his death in 1971, many well-known musical personalities, such as Marion Anderson, and other friends gathered at the Salon Methodist Church in New York City for a program entitled "A Musical Tribute to Hall Johnson." Most of the music was composed by Johnson himself, including songs for adults and children, choral selections, and a cantata.

The plaque in Athens City Hall honoring Johnson and his birthplace was placed there in 1976, five years after his death, by several national music organizations which wished to continue to honor Hall Johnson's memory. But like all great musicians, Hall Johnson will always live on in his music.

William A. Pledger

THE BLACK JOURNALISTS

Current Events and Controversy

We wish to plead our own cause.
Too long have others spoken for us.
Too long has the publick
been deceived by misrepresentations,
in things which concern us dearly....

FREEDOM'S JOURNAL, *1827*
America's first black newspaper

Before and immediately following the turn of the twentieth century, five black newspapers were born in Athens. They thrived intermittently for about forty years. Then the black press was silent again until the *Athens Voice* was heard in 1975.

It all began in 1879 with the *Athens Blade*, which published religious and social news about blacks in Athens and some surrounding counties, in addition to substantial amounts of national news. This twenty-five-cent weekly had a surprisingly large circulation: it was distributed in several northern cities, including New York and Washington, D.C., as well as about twenty-five cities and towns throughout Georgia.

The *Blade* was doubtless named for its ability to cut when necessary. Neither of its outspoken editors shrank from controversy. In fact, they welcomed opportunities to rail against any form of injustice. Here, for example, is an excerpt from one of William Henry Heard's fiery editorials:

> These prejudiced white men do all they can against schools, so that they may be able to cheat the ignorant colored man out of his wages and to keep him ignorant so that they may keep him poor. Young colored men, are you willing these things should continue—I am willing to die for liberty and every man that has a heart should be.

A closely contested municipal election campaign raged the year the Blade was founded. The paper endorsed mayoral candidate J.H. Carlton whose slogan was "Free Schools for Everybody," and openly condemned his opponent, a Mr. Talmadge.

In spite of its bellicose style, both black and white merchants advertised in the *Blade*. J.C. Wilkins touted the virtues of his $8.50 coal-burning stove on the same page where former slave Ike Derricotte advertised his boot and shoemaking establishment on Jackson Street. That issue also carried Atlanta University's announcement of registration for the fall term. It advised prospective black students: "Tuition in common English branches one dollar, and in higher branches two dollars a month."

Elsewhere in the paper you would have seen an ad for Smith's Worm Oil suggesting, "If your child has no appetite and is restless at night, give him a dose of worm oil and relieve him." In those days before the FDA and the consumer movement, "the greatest worm oil ever discovered (with) over twenty-five thousand bottles sold to one honse [sic] in five months" was among the many quick cures which appeared in the *Blade* as well as other papers of that era.

The *Blade's* popularity doubtless had a lot to do with the fact that it was published by two well-known activists. Both men were staunch proponents of equal rights for blacks, although each man pursued his goal in his own way.

Col. William A. Pledger was described in his obituary as "one of the most unique and forceful characters that have moulded public sentiment for more than a quarter century." His coeditor, William Henry Heard, was equally unique and forceful. He had to flee to Athens in the late 1870s to take refuge from angry whites in South Carolina who objected to his winning a seat in the legislature.

Pledger was a lawyer, best known for his political talents. He served as a delegate to every national Republican convention from 1876 to 1900, and was honored four successive times by being selected as a delegate at large from the state.

As early as 1876 when he attended his first convention, the Athens Georgian, a white newspaper, described Pledger as "one of the shrewdest leaders of the Republican Party in this part of the state." Four years later he was elected chairman of the Republican State Central Committee of Georgia—the first black man to serve in that important post. However, his attempt to become Clarke County's third black legislator failed eight years later.

At the first meeting of the Afro-American League in 1890, Pledger made what many of his contemporaries considered a "militant" address by "declaring that disobedience to the constitution was at the bottom of the race question" in the racially segregated South. Five years later he shared the speaker's platform at the Atlanta Cotton Exposition with Dr. Booker T. Washington, founder of Tuskegee Institute in Alabama.

The exposition was the site of Washington's famous address in which he urged blacks to "cast down your buckets where you are" and to seek economic parity rather than social equality with southern whites. Although Pledger would later adopt Washington's conciliatory philosophy, in 1895 he assumed a more demanding posture concerning the rights of American blacks. He told the exposition audience, "The Afro-American asks only for justice. He knows that he is entitled to that much ... and it is his duty to ask for it."

Pledger risked his life on several occasions to back up his opinions on civil rights. Once he led a group of armed men to the Athens jail to rescue two black men, who had shot and killed a white university student, from the clutches of an angry lynch mob.

A native of Jonesboro, Pledger was born in the 1850s and died in Atlanta in 1904. A writer for the newspaper *Colored American* summed up his life this way:

> As a journalist, he wielded a fearless and trenchant pen, and was among the first to edit a paper in his native state. He...attended all the national conventions and [was] a potent factor in directing the course of thought that emanated from the colored press for thirty years.

Frederick Douglass, the prominent abolitionist, credited Pledger with possessing the unique qualities of mind that make men great. He predicted, "In the future, the hope of the race would come from the South," because of the achievements of men like Pledger.

Pledger's cohort, William Henry Heard, was also a native Georgian who was born a slave in Elberton in 1850. He moved to South Carolina at the age of twenty-three, taught school in Mt. Carmel, and attended the University of South Carolina for two years.

At twenty-six he won a seat in the legislature, but an outraged white citizenry refused to let him serve his term. He therefore fled to Athens where he set up a school for black children in the basement of Pierce's Chapel African Methodist Episcopal Church in 1876. That same year, Heard met Pledger when he began to study law under his tutelage.

In 1879—the year he helped found the *Blade* – Heard was converted to the Methodist faith. He abandoned his study of law to devote himself to studying for the ministry and helping edit the newspaper. Four years later, shortly before the *Blade* ceased publication, Heard left Athens to assume the pastorate of a Methodist church in Aiken, South Carolina.

He was later assigned to the Bethel Church, the African Methodist Episcopal mother church in Philadelphia. By 1908, at the age of fifty-eight, Heard was ordained the thirty-fifth bishop of the A.M.E. Church, a position he held for twenty-nine years until he died at the age of eighty-seven at his home in Philadelphia. He was appointed ambassador to Liberia by President Grover Cleveland, and established a church there.

The *Athens Blade* was a short-lived newspaper. Only one year after it was founded, Pledger changed its name to the *Atlanta Defiant* and moved it to Atlanta. He brought the paper back to Athens two years later, but it lasted only a year or two more. Heard and his "radical pen" moved to South Carolina in 1883, and the following year the *Blade* disappeared from the scene.

Athens was without a black newspaper for only three years until the first copy of the *Athens Clipper* came off the press in 1887. Its editor, S.B. Davis, continued to publish the four-page weekly for at least twenty years from his office at 116 East Clayton Street where the main office of Bank of America is now located.

Billed as "the only colored paper published in northeast Georgia," the *Clipper* had a weekly circulation of seven hundred copies. A one-year subscription cost $1.25, or about 3¢ a copy. Unlike its predecessor, it confined itself to religious news and other strictly local events in the black community.

THE ATHENS CLIPPER.

BY S. B. DAVIS. ATHENS, GA., SATURDAY, AUG. 31, 1901. VOL. 14. NO. 17.

Athens Clipper

On page one of a typical issue, a letter from a correspondent in Comer tells of a "sad occurrence"—the fatal shooting of an old black man named Jarrels by a white man named Moore. While Jarrels lay on his deathbed:

> He was shot three more times by Moore's brother who went to Deacon Jarrels's house ... shot fifteen times in the house ... shooting Deacon Jarrels's wife's finger off.

The report concludes with a warning that the Moore brothers were still on the loose and were allegedly looking for another old man and his wife, intending to shoot both of them on sight.

More routine was a report by editor Davis of a meeting of the Savannah River Baptist Association in Middleton, Georgia. Davis praised the quality of the sermons delivered at the convention, then added, "The *Clipper* man was kindly treated by the whole association, and especially the ladies."

The *Clipper* advertised the Uptown Barber Shop's fifteen-cent haircuts, the South Atlantic Railway Line's schedules, and S.L. Hicklin's Newtown Colored Enterprise-Grocery Store. The latter promised potential customers that Hicklin "will sell to you cheap for cash, give you your money's worth, and treat you white."

Following Davis' death, his widow, Minnie Davis, published the *Clipper* for a short period of time and then sold the newspaper to A.T. Jackson around 1912. Unfortunately, few copies of this newspaper are in existence today. The only known copies were found by the author in the possession of Rosa Mae Strickland, a retired teacher in Athens. They were subsequently presented to the Special Collections section of the University of Georgia Library.

Even less is known about *Progressive Era*, the third of Athens' five black newspapers. We do know it was published by W.D. Johnson, D.D., a Methodist bishop, and W.H. Harris, a black doctor (see chapter 7). While its predecessors emphasized political and religious events, the *Progressive*

Era was apparently interested mainly in more and better education for its black readers.

By 1914 Monroe Bowers "Pink" Morton, a local black entrepreneur, had purchased the *Era* and was serving as its publisher and editor. Almost nothing is known about Morton's journalistic career, principally because not one copy of the *Progressive Era* published during his editorship is extant. But his success in the business world and his activities as a political power broker within the national Republican party are well documented.

In 1914, the *Athens Daily Herald* described the three-year-old Morton Building in downtown Athens as the "largest building of its kind owned exclusively by a colored man in the world." Morton owned the four-story building as well as twenty-five or thirty other houses in Athens.

Morton was born in 1856, the son of a slave mother, Elizabeth Morgan, and a prominent white man, and began his business career at the age of six. What he lacked in formal education (he had very little), he made up in motivation. From his first important job as hotel porter he went into the contracting business on a small scale. It wasn't long before he turned it into a profitable business. "Without friends to back him or in any way to encourage him, but with indomitable energy, thrift, and industry [Morton] forced his way through every obstacle," according to the *Daily Herald*.

Morton retired from the contracting business temporarily in 1897 in order to accept the appointment of postmaster of the city of Athens—the second black man in Athens history to hold this prestigious position. He and former state legislator Madison Davis had sought the position, but Morton won the appointment largely on the strength of the publicity he received by having his picture published in the *New York World*.

Morton had the added distinction of serving as a delegate to the 1896 Republican National Convention, and was subsequently elected to the committee that notified William McKinley of his selection as the GOP presidential candidate. Morton's daughter Maude also recalled being told that her father went to Washington, D.C. in January, 1897 to participate in the inaugural activities following McKinley's presidential victory.

Monroe B. Morton

During his five-year tenure as postmaster in Athens, Morton instituted many progressive reforms and improvements. When his term was up, the forty-three-year-old Morton went back to the business world with renewed enthusiasm. Investing large amounts of capital in land and building construction, Morton became one of the richest, most influential black men in Georgia and the Southeast.

The courthouse at Washington, Georgia and the government building in Anniston, Alabama are among the prominent buildings he financed or constructed. In Athens, his home town, he built a ten-thousand-dollar marble building on Clayton Street, as well as the Morton Building on the corner of Hull and Washington streets.

Opening in 1910, the Morton Building housed the offices of doctors and black-owned businesses, as well as the performance hall, the Morton Theatre. Often described as the "colored opera house" the Morton was a showplace for cultural performances by local and traveling artists, state professional meetings, graduation ceremonies, and traveling vaudeville troupes. It hosted all the famous names in black entertainment, including "Shuffle Along," a popular black musical of the early 1920s that played a year on Broadway. After the performance at the Morton, the production played Athens' "white opera house," the Colonial Theatre.

Even after the Morton Theatre was renovated in the thirties so patrons could see silent movies and, later on, talking pictures, big stars such as Cab Callaway, Duke Ellington, and Louis Armstrong still occasionally visited its stage.

The four-story retail and office building, surrounded by multi-story lodge halls which have since been razed, was for years the center for all important gatherings in the African-American community. For example, local black schools held their annual operettas in the theater in May. But the observance of the anniversary of the Emancipation Proclamation on January 1 of each year was the most important annual event held at the Morton Building, which became a proud symbol of the power and wealth of Athens's black middle class.

The last live performance was in 1944, and a fire closed the theater portion of the building in 1950. It continued to house black businesses until it was renovated as a community performing arts facility in the 1990s.

The first black newspaper to be founded in Athens after the turn of the century was *The Athens Republic.* This paper filled the journalistic void that was created in the Athens black community after the *Clipper* and *Era* disappeared from the newsstands around 1920. The Republic was published for an unknown length of time by a black minister whose office was located on Hancock Avenue in the Callaway Building.

Another black newspaper, the *Athens Republique*, may have been related in some way with the *Republic*. First published in November of 1919, the *Republique* was printed in Athens for at least four years. According to its motto, the eight-page paper was "Devoted to the Religious, the Educational and the Industrial Development of the Colored Race." The paper and its editor, Julian L. Brown, were closely associated with the Jeruel Baptist Association and Jeruel Baptist Institute.

Touting itself as "Small but Newsy," the *Republique* carried a variety of stories about black religious and social affairs in its November 3, 1923, edition. The lead story in this issue concerned the annual meeting of the Order of Good Samaritans in Hawkinsville, Georgia on October 24th of that year. The nearly two hundred delegates who attended the convention were addressed by Professor H.A. Hunt, principal of Fort Valley High and Industrial School. The reporter noted:

> The business sessions of [the] Grand Lodge showed great progress and improvement in their methods of legislating and in the handling of business. Not one time in the whole of the sessions did the body become disorderly or unruly.

Another story urged readers to "Remember The 'Colored Boys of'18.'" A mass rally in honor of black World War I veterans was scheduled for the following Sunday at Union Baptist Institute. The *Republique* editorialized,

> If the dominant race has failed to keep its pledges to these men; if they have accorded them even less consideration than they did before the war, let us—their own flesh and blood—show these men all the honor due to blood-stained warriors who returned from the battlefields with palms of victory in their hands.

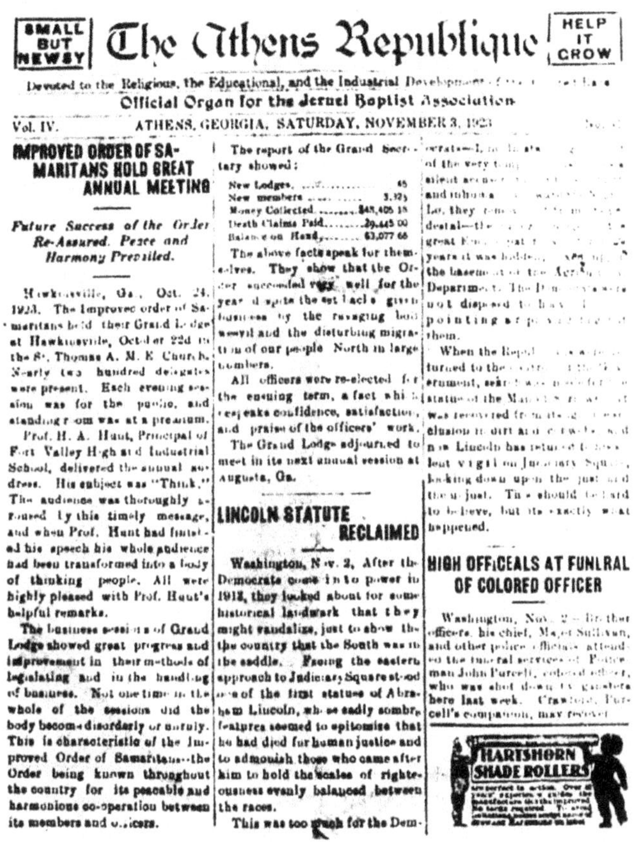

SMALL BUT NEWSY | **The Athens Republique** | HELP IT GROW

Devoted to the Religious, the Educational, and the Industrial Development [illegible]

Official Organ for the Jeruel Baptist Association

Vol. IV. ATHENS, GEORGIA, SATURDAY, NOVEMBER 3, 1923 [illegible]

IMPROVED ORDER OF SAMARITANS HOLD GREAT ANNUAL MEETING

Future Success of the Order Re-Assured. Peace and Harmony Prevailed.

Hawkinsville, Ga., Oct. 24, 1923. The Improved order of Samaritans held their Grand Lodge at Hawkinsville, October 22d in the St. Thomas A. M. E. Church. Nearly two hundred delegates were present. Each evening session was for the public, and standing room was at a premium.

Prof. H. A. Hunt, Principal of Fort Valley High and Industrial School, delivered the annual address. His subject was "Think." The audience was thoroughly aroused by this timely message, and when Prof. Hunt had finished his speech his whole audience had been transformed into a body of thinking people. All were highly pleased with Prof. Hunt's helpful remarks.

The business sessions of Grand Lodge showed great progress and improvement in their methods of legislating and in the handling of business. Not one time in the whole of the sessions did the body become disorderly or unruly. This is characteristic of the Improved Order of Samaritans—the Order being known throughout the country for its peacable and harmonious co-operation between its members and officers.

The report of the Grand Secretary showed:

New Lodges	45
New members	3,325
Money Collected	$45,405 18
Death Claims Paid	29,445 00
Balance on Hand	63,077 66

The above facts speak for themselves. They show that the Order succeeded very well for the year despite the set backs given business by the ravaging boll weevil and the disturbing migration of our people North in large numbers.

All officers were re-elected for the ensuing term, a fact which bespeaks confidence, satisfaction, and praise of the officers' work.

The Grand Lodge adjourned to meet in its next annual session at Augusta, Ga.

LINCOLN STATUTE RECLAIMED

Washington, Nov. 2, After the Democrats came into power in 1913, they looked about for some historical landmark that they might vandalize, just to show the country that the South was in the saddle. Facing the eastern approach to Judiciary Square stood one of the first statues of Abraham Lincoln, whose sadly sombre features seemed to epitomize that he had died for human justice and to admonish those who came after him to hold the scales of righteousness evenly balanced between the races.

This was too much for the Democrats—[illegible] of the very [illegible] silent accuser [illegible] and inhuman [illegible] Lo, they [illegible] destal—the [illegible] great [illegible] years it was hidden [illegible] the basement of the [illegible] Department. The Democrats were not disposed to have [illegible] pointing [illegible] them.

When the Republicans returned to the control of the government, search was made for the statue of the Martyr [illegible] was recovered from its [illegible] seclusion in dirt and cobwebs, and now Lincoln has returned to his silent vigil on Judiciary Square, looking down upon the just and the unjust. This should be hard to believe, but its exactly what happened.

HIGH OFFICEALS AT FUNLRAL OF COLORED OFFICER

Washington, Nov. 2 — Brother officers, his chief, Major Sullivan, and other police officials attended the funeral services of Policeman John Purcell, colored officer, who was shot down by gangsters here last week. Crawford, Purcell's companion, may recover

HARTSHORN SHADE ROLLERS [illegible]

Athens Republique

The paper featured a lodge and church directory along with the inevitable advertisements. The Nemo Self-Reducing Corset Company proclaimed, "Good News for Stout Women." Their three-dollar corsets were real bargains, according to the ad. On that same page, Madam Lela Wright, a "Poro Hair Dresser," asked readers to come to her hair salon in the Morton Building.

Fred O. Smith (left) and Rick Dunn

Editor Julian Brown also advertised himself as a licensed notary public and a "Maker of All Kinds of Legal Papers." Beneath this solicitation, Mrs. Mary Causey of 89D Carr Street announced the availability of her "Scalp Curing" and "Smokeless Hair Treatment." Finally, an apparently new product called Musterole was said to "do all the work of the old-fashioned mustard plaster—without the blister." According to the ad, Musterole would give prompt relief from "bronchitis, sore throat, coughs, colds, croup, neuralgia, headache, congestion, rheumatism, sprains, sore muscles, bruises, and all aches and pains."

Following the demise of the *Republique,* there was no black newspaper to take its place until June 12, 1975 when the *Athens Voice* was founded by two students, Fred O. Smith and Michael L. Thurmond. They conceived the idea of a black newspaper while both were in their senior year at Paine College in Augusta. Less than a month after their graduation and return to Athens, the weekly *Athens Voice* was being sold on the streets for twenty-five cents a copy.

In the front-page lead editorial in the inaugural issue of the newspaper, the editors stated that the *Voice* "has bridged a communicative chasm which has existed in the city of Athens" since the *Athens Republique* ceased publication during the mid-1920s. The editorial also highlighted the fact that the *Voice* grew out of the long-expressed need for a newspaper in Athens "of, for and by black people."

Published by J. Lowell Ware of Atlanta, the *Voice* featured a variety of national, state, and local news items, as well as editorial opinions. Rick Dunn and Harold Moon were members of the editorial staff.

Black journalism had another first not long after the *Voice* was launched. *Image* magazine, published and edited by Robert Harrison, was the first magazine ever published by a black man for black readers in Athens. The first issue appeared in February 1976.

More than one hundred years have passed since the first black newspaper was published in Athens in 1879. Throughout this period, black editors and publishers of the various news organs have informed and entertained their readers, while they pleaded the cause of the traditionally voiceless segments of the greater Athens community. Armed with the printed word, the Heards, Pledgers, Davises, and Smiths have been in the vanguard of movements to bring political and social equality to all the people of northeast Georgia.

William Henry Heard

The *Athens Voice* ceased publication in 1977, lapsing while Thurmond attended law school and Smith earned a graduate degree in journalism from the University of Georgia. In 1980, Smith attempted a revival of the *Voice*, with four totally local special editions. In a front-page editorial, Smith stated:

> In this era of widespread integration, we are constantly confronted with the necessity for black institutions to justify their Existence... But as long as there is acute disparity in traditional media's coverage, understanding and employment, the urgent and pressing need for the black press shall remain intact.

He added, that despite data indicating that the white media portray unrealistic views of blacks and lack an appreciation and understanding of black history and culture, "these same media are relied upon to express and discuss the concerns of blacks and other minorities." The last issue, on July 29, 1980, strongly endorsed candidates for state and local office, adding, "... if, like many fear, our ruin will be caused as a result of our involvement in some essential political matters, let history record that we, too, took a stand."

The *Voice* was replaced by the *Athens Courier*, published by Rick Dunn and Harold Moon, from 1982 until about 1985. Dunn, another UGA journalism graduate has been a contributing columnist to African-American publications and to Athens Newspapers, Inc. for more than 20 years. In the 1990s, roughly from 1994 until 1998 or 1999, the monthly *Griot Messenger* was published by Jim Rhinehart.

Image Magazine discontinued publication around 1980. In 1993, Walter Allen Jr. began publishing bimonthly *Zebra Magazine*, still a source of news, features and history about Athens' African-American Community. Allen sporadically publishes a newspaper, *The Athens Tribune*. Another publication, the *Athens Minority Telephone Book*, is published by Charlie Monroe and Youth Entrepreneur Services, Inc.

Since 1978, Athens has had two radio stations, WXAG-AM 1470 and WBKZ-AM 880. The former began programming for the Athens' black community in 1982, when attorney and University of Georgia law professor Larry Blount organized a company with principal investors Evelyn Corene Neely, Mack Benton, Ed Wilker and Michael Thurmond who purchased station WDOL, converting it to African-American programming. After experiencing some financial difficulty, it ceased operation around 1988, to be supplanted by Stan Carter's WBKZ. This station began black programming in 1992.

Dr. Bradford Brown purchased WBKZ in 1994, upgraded equipment, and increased coverage to 23 counties. Managed by Melvin Jeter, the station features music and news, religious programs, gospel, jazz, and community forums. In 2001, Thurmond returned WXAG to the airways and added an FM signal. The station, which promotes itself as the "Heart and Soul of Athens," is currently the only African-American owned radio station in northeast Georgia.

Fred Smith currently serves as the president of the Athens Chapter of the National Association for the Advancement of Colored People. According to Smith, minority owned media has played a critical role in the history of black Athens. He stated, "There are critical issues in the black community that are often overlooked by the general media. Minority journalists and their media have always been and will continue to be extremely important in our struggle to secure equal justice in America."

Michael L. Thurmond

ABOUT THE AUTHOR

Update—Third Edition

Michael L. Thurmond's accomplishments over the past forty years have far exceeded the predictions made in the first edition of this book, which seemed wildly inflated at the time. Raised in Clarke County, Georgia, this son of a sharecropper graduated with honors from Paine College with a degree in philosophy and religion, and received a Juris Doctor degree from the University of South Carolina, before the publication of *A Story Untold, Black Men and Women in Athens History*. He later completed the Political Executives program at the John F. Kennedy School of Government at Harvard University.

A short four years after law school and returning to Athens to establish a law practice, Thurmond launched a campaign for state representative from Clarke County. Although not successful, he was not deterred and returned to the political arena two years later to try again. The result was another loss. Although most people would have quit after two straight losses, Thurmond would not walk away from his goal and returned two years later for a third run; his perseverance paid off. In 1986, Thurmond became the first African-American elected to the Georgia General Assembly from Clarke County since Reconstruction. While in the legislature

Thurmond authored major legislation providing more than $250 million in tax relief to Georgia's senior citizens and working families.

Thurmond next received a gubernatorial appointment to lead the state Division of Family and Children Services and directed Georgia's historic transition from welfare to work. He created the innovative Work First program, which helped more than 90,000 welfare-dependent Georgia families move from dependence into the workforce.

In 1997, Thurmond became a distinguished lecturer at the University of Georgia's Carl Vinson Institute of Government. The following year he was elected Georgia labor commissioner, becoming the first African-American elected to a statewide office without prior appointment. During his three terms as labor commissioner, Thurmond's most significant achievement was the construction of a $20 million school for children with disabilities at the Roosevelt Warm Springs Institute.

Thurmond's challenges continued when he next served as superintendent of DeKalb County, Georgia public schools. He is credited with stabilizing the school system during a governance crisis, upgrading its threatened accreditation, eliminating a multimillion-dollar deficit and improving student academic performance and graduation rates.

Thurmond's list of accomplishments was still not complete. He won a landslide victory in 2016 to become chief executive officer of DeKalb County, one of the most diverse counties in the Southeast. Since being sworn-in, Thurmond's primary mission has been restoring trust in county government. Other priorities he has pursued as CEO include adopting a balanced budget, offering summer youth employment, and improving employee compensation.

Thurmond's accomplishments in fundamentally transforming the culture and enhancing operations of complex government organizations such as the Georgia Division of Family and Children Services, the Georgia Department of Labor, the DeKalb County School District and DeKalb County government have resulted in his being widely recognized as a "turnaround expert."

In addition to *A Story Untold,* Thurmond has authored *Freedom: Georgia's Antislavery Heritage, 1733-1865* (Atlanta, GA: Longstreet Press, 2002), which received the Georgia Historical Society's Lilla Hawes Ward award. In 2004, the Georgia Center for the Book listed *Freedom* as one of the 25 Books All Georgian's Should Read. Thurmond currently serves on the University of Georgia Libraries Board of Visitors and is presently finishing a third book on Georgia history, which promises a new world-view of Georgia's founding father.

Where will Thurmond's impact next be felt? No one has the foresight to make that prediction. But what can be said is that Thurmond is and will continue to be a role model for both today's youth and the youth of tomorrow. The story of his life is the quintessential example of how a good education, hard work and perseverance brings results.

—Dan A. Aldridge, Jr.
Athens Historical Society, Board
February 2019

ABOUT MIKE THURMOND *[First Edition]*

Mike Thurmond has made quite a bit of history in twenty-five years.

The youngest of nine children, he grew up in a close, supportive family in Athens. For eleven years he attended all-black schools until, in his senior year, he entered newly consolidated Clarke Central High School.

It was a year of turbulence and adjustments, but Mike Thurmond emerged as co-president of the student council, co-holder of the 100-yard-dash record, member of the football team, and one of the speakers at his graduation ceremonies.

On to Paine College, where he majored in philosophy and religion while demonstrating his ability to be a mover and shaper of events. He started a newspaper designed to reflect students' views more accurately than the college paper. It later became the newsletter of the student government association and, the following year, Thurmond became editor of the official student newspaper. Meanwhile, he wrote obituaries for a black weekly, the *Augusta News Review*, and eventually moved up to police reporting.

Although he shuns typewriters, Thurmond always ends up writing or publishing something. But he likes directing things even better. During his two years as president of the student government at Paine, he set up a student court system and initiated the Augusta People's Project. Energized by his leadership, Paine students tutored adults and children, worked with juvenile offenders, encouraged voter registration, and staged Feed-the-People concerts before Thanksgiving and Christmas in behalf of the poor.

For his outstanding leadership, the student government association awarded Thurmond the title of president emeritus— the first time such an honor has been bestowed. And for his academic diligence, Paine College awarded him his bachelor of arts degree cum laude. Small wonder, then, that Thurmond was listed in *Who's Who in American Colleges and Universities*, or that he was voted Outstanding Student by Omega Psi Phi, and Student of the Year by Kappa Alpha Psi.

During the summer between his graduation from Paine and his enrollment in law school, Thurmond returned home to help launch the *Athens Voice*, a newspaper by and for black Athenians. Now in his final year at the South Carolina Law Center, Thurmond is still indulging his penchant for writing and directing things. He helped found the *Advocate*, official newsletter of the Black American Law Students Association, and presides over the association's South Carolina chapter as president this year. He also finds time to work as a law clerk in the Fifth Judicial Circuit Solicitor's Office in Columbia.

What's next? Thurmond says he'll return to Athens to open a law office and write. His articles about black history and current events have already appeared in the *Athens Banner-Herald*, *Daily News*, *Observer*, and

Voice. No doubt he'll write more books, too. No one really worries about Mike Thurmond. If an outlet for his zest and talents doesn't exist, he'll create one.

—Dorothy Sparer
Editor of the First Edition 1978

ACKNOWLEDGMENTS

The author expresses his heartfelt thanks once again to those mentioned in the first and second editions of *A Story Untold* who made this book possible through their cooperation and support: the Athens-Clarke Heritage Foundation, the Athens Clarke County Bicentennial Steering Committee, and the invaluable assistance of Judy Long and Anne Richmond Boston of Hill Street Press. Thanks also to those previously acknowledged who helped in gathering information: Wilucia Green, Fred O. Smith Sr., Milton Hill, Dr. John Davis, Dr. Farris Johnson, Jr., Nathaniel Fox, Vernon Payne, Katie Hampton, Kim Callaway, Rick Dunn, Barbara McRae, Gwen Moon Wright, Marvin J. Nunnally, Linda Edwards, Frances McBride, Nelson Morgan and other staff at the UGA Hargrett Rare Book and Manuscript Library, Laura Carter of Athens Regional Library, and Cheryl Phillips of the Clarke County Board of Education.

The author is also indebted to publisher Al Hester and editor Conoly Hester for their dedication, perseverance and hard work in bringing the second edition to completion and to Deeds Publishing and its staff for their dedication, perseverance and hard work in bringing the third edition to completion. Last, but by no means least, thanks to Athens Historical Society for its vision in seeing the need for a third edition and for its work in bringing this edition to completion. This organization is to be commended for its dedication and work over many decades to preserve the history of Athens-Clarke County and to enlighten the community on the richness of that history.

—Michael L. Thurmond
February 2019

NOTES ON SOURCES

Because an abundance of footnotes on the printed page would interrupt the reading of this material, the author used a considerable amount of internal documentation. For this reason, we would like to call attention to sources in this section—particularly those that were especially helpful and informative. We hope this will aid students and others who wish to continue research on the history of black men and women in Athens and Clarke County.

JUBILEE!

Robert Gamble's thesis, entitled "Athens: The Study of a Georgia Town During Reconstruction," was especially helpful in recreating the period that immediately followed the emancipation of northeast Georgia slaves. Newspaper accounts from the *Southern Watchman* supplied some interesting insights into the attitudes and opinions of white Athenians during that period. But researchers must bear in mind that most of the newspaper stories are affected by the racial prejudices of their authors. The eye witness accounts of former slaves added color and balance to this particular chapter. The most valuable volume of slave narratives was

The American Slave, volume 12, which was compiled by writers working through the Federal Writers Project of the mid-1930s.

Bennett, Lerone, Jr. "Jubilee," *Ebony Magazine*, 59, February 1972, pp.37-46.

Conway, Alan. *The Reconstruction of Georgia*. Minneapolis: University of Minnesota Press, 1966.

Coulter, Ellis Merton. *College Life in the Old South*. 2nd rev. ed. Athens: University of Georgia Press, 1951.Gamble, Robert. "Athens: The Study of a Georgia Town During Reconstruction." Master's thesis, University of Georgia, 1967.

Hull, Augustus L. *Annals of Athens 1801-1901*. Athens, 1906.

Killion, Ronald, *Slavery Time When I Was Chillun Down on Marsters Plantation*. New York: Beehive Press, 1969.

Rawick, George P., ed. *The American Slave*. Vol. 12. Ga. Narratives, Part 1 & 2. Westport, Conn: Greenwood Publishing Co., 1972.

The *New York World*. October 7, 1865.

Shadgett, Olive Hall. *The Republican Party in Georgia: From Reconstruction Through 1900*. Athens: University of Georgia Press, 1964.

Southern Banner. September 6,1865.*Southern Watchman*. May 24, 1865, July 26, 1865, February 7, 1866.

The War of Rebellion: A Compilation of the Official Records of the Union and Confederate Armies, Series 1. Vol. 49. Washington.

TWO LAWMAKERS

Information about the personal lives of Alfred Richardson and Madison Davis is scarce, but Gamble's thesis on Reconstruction Athens was helpful, as were some local newspaper accounts from that period. Richardson's testimony in the Congressional Record is enlightening in regard to the nature of the political atmosphere in Athens during his tenure in the

Georgia Legislature. By far the most comprehensive study of Georgia's black Reconstruction legislators is Ethel Maude Christler's Atlanta University thesis entitled "Participation of Negroes in the Government of Georgia 1867-1870."

Angell, Stephen Ward, *Bishop Henry McNeal Turner and African-American Religion in the South*. Knoxville: The University of Tennessee Press, 1992.

Athens Banner Watchman. October 3, 1882.

Athens Northeast Georgian. October 4, 1872.

Atlanta Constitution. July 4, 1868 through September 5, 1868.

Coulter, Ellis Merton. *Negro Legislators in Georgia During the Reconstruction Period*. Athens: University of Georgia Press, 1968.

Christler, Ethel Maude. "Participation of Negroes in the Government of Georgia 1867-1870." Master's thesis, Atlanta University, 1932

Gamble, Robert. "The Study of a Georgia Town During Reconstruction." Master's thesis, University of Georgia, 1967.

Hull, Augustus L *Annals of Athens, 1801-1901*. Athens, 1906.

Journals of the Georgia House of Representatives, 1868-1872.

Report of the Congressional Committee Investigating the Activities of the Ku Klux Klan in the South.

Shadgett, Olive Hall. *The Republican Party in Georgia: From Reconstruction through 1900*. Athens: University of Georgia Press, 1964. *Southern Watchman*. April 29,1868 and October 9,1872.

THE BLACK CHURCH

Researching this chapter was particularly difficult because few of the local black churches have compiled or published church histories.

The Phelps-Stokes studies provided only a sketchy picture of the black churches in Athens and in the rural areas of Clarke County.

Athens Banner-Herald Church of the Week, Mar. 1976

Barton, William E. *Old Plantation Hymns*. New York: AMS Press, 1972.

Dubois, W.E.B. *The Souls of Black Folk*. Millwood, NY: Krans-Thomson Organization, 1973.

Gamble, Robert. "Athens: The Study of Georgia Towns During Reconstruction." Master's thesis, University of Georgia, 1967.

Hynds, Ernest. *Antebellum Athens and Clarke County, Georgia*. Athens: University of Georgia Press, 1974.

Killion, Ronald. *Slavery Time When I Was Chillun Down on Marsters Plantation*. New York: Beehive Press, 1969.

Locke, Alain. *The Negro and His Music*. New York: Arno Press and the New York Times Press, 1968.

Locke, Alain. *Negro Art Past and Present*. New York: Arno Press and the New York Times Press, 1968.

McCoy, Rowena. "The History of Ebenezer Baptist Church." Mimeographed.

Mell, E.B. "Reminiscences of Athens, Georgia about 1800-1900." Master's thesis, University of Georgia, 1956.

Northeast Georgian, October 4, 1872.

Phelps-Stokes Fellowship Studies. Woofter, T.J., "The Negroes of Athens, Ga." No. 1, *University of Georgia Bulletin*, Vol. 14, no. 4. Athens: University of Georgia, 1913.

Phelps-Stokes Fellowship Studies. Hill, Walter Barnard, "Rural Survey of Clarke County, Georgia." No. 2, *University of Georgia Bulletin* Vol. 15, no. 3. Athens: University of Georgia, 1915.

Schinkel, Peter. "The Negro in Athens and Clarke County." Master's thesis, University of Georgia, 1971. *Southern Watchman*, April 29, 1868.

Southern Watchman, October 9, 1872.

National Register Nomination for First A.M.E. Church, Dec. 27,1979

EDUCATORS AND THEIR SCHOOLS

Coulter's *College Life in the Old South* presented a somewhat detailed account of the early movement to establish a school for blacks in Athens. But the majority of the information about Knox Institute and Union Baptist Institute was gathered from school catalogs and interviews with local alumni of the institutions. Two Phelps-Stokes Fund studies provided important statistics about the private and public black schools in Athens and rural Clarke County during the early part of the twentieth century.

The 1933 edition of *Who's Who in Colored America* contained background material on Judia Harris. This information was supplemented by interviews with some of her former students. *Negro Education Private and Higher Schools For Colored People*, edited by Thomas Jones, was also helpful in developing this chapter. A valuable unpublished source was Rosa Strickland's private scrapbook collection. Much was also gained from studying the *Athens City School Reports* at the Clarke County Board of Education.

Athens Banner-Herald, Sept. 3,1963.

Athens Banner-Herald. April 17-20, 1970.

Athens City School Directories.

Athens Clipper. August 31,1901.

Athens Voice, June 28, 1975.

Conway, Alan. *The Reconstruction of Georgia.* Minneapolis: University of Minnesota Press, 1966.

Coulter, Ellis Merton. *College Life in the Old South.* 2nd rev. ed. Athens: University of Georgia Press, 1951.

Gamble, Robert. "Athens: The Study of a Georgia Town During Reconstruction." Master's thesis, University of Georgia, 1967.

Heard, William H. *From Slavery to the Bishopric in the A.M.E. Church.* New York: the New York Times Press, 1969.

Hartshorn, W.N. editor, *An Era of Progress and Promise: 1863-1910.* Boston: The Priscilla Publishing Company.
Hull, Augustus L. *Annals of Athens, 1801-1901.* Athens, 1906.
Jones, Thomas Jesse, ed. *Negro Education Private and Higher Schools For Colored People in the U.S.* New York: Arno Press and the New York Times Press, 1969.
Knox Herald. May 1925 and May 1914.Phelps-Stokes Fellowship Studies. Woofter, T.J., "The Negroes of Athens, Ga." No. 1. *University of Georgia Bulletin*, Vol. 14, no. 4. Athens: University of Georgia, 1913.
Phelps-Stokes Fellowship Studies. Hill, Walter Barnard. "Rural Survey of Clarke County, Georgia." No. 2, *University of Georgia Bulletin*, Vol. 15, no. 3. Athens: University of Georgia, 1915.
Schinkel, Peter Evans. "The Negro in Athens and Clarke County." Master's thesis, University of Georgia, 1971.
Sessoms, Josie B., chairman of writing committee. *Jeanes Supervision in Georgia Schools: A Guiding Light in Education.* The Georgia Association of Jeanes Curriculum Directors in Cooperation with Southern Education Foundation, 1975.
Southern Watchman. January 9, 1867.
Strickland, Rosa. Private scrapbook collection.
Trillin, Calvin. *An Education in Georgia: The Integration of Charlayne Hunter and Hamilton Holmes.* New York: Viking Press, 1964.
Union Baptist Institute Catalogue. 1935.

SAMUEL F. HARRIS

Many of the same sources used in Chapter 4 are also relevant here.

Athens Daily Herald. Special edition, 1911.
Athens Banner-Herald, July 2,1935*Athens Banner-Herald*, Feb. 2,1983.

Article by Michael Thurmond, with assistance by Fred O. Smith and Janice Mathis.

The Black Mammy Memorial Institute Brochure. Special Collections, University of Georgia Library.

Who's Who in Colored America. Brooklyn, N.Y.: Who's Who in Colored America, Thomas Yenser, editor, third edition. 1933.

MEDICAL PIONEERS

Athens Daily Herald. Special edition, 1914.

Athens Voice, June 1980 and July 1980.

Curtis, James. *Blacks, Medical Schools, and Society.* Ann Arbor: The University of Michigan Press, 1971.

Gordon, Asa. *The Georgia Negro: A History*. Spartanburg, S.C.: The Reprint Co., 1937.

Morais, Herbert M. *The History of the Negro in Medicine*. The International Library of Negro Life and History. New York: Publishers Company, 1968.

HALL JOHNSON

The majority of the information used in this section was taken from an excellent article in the 1945 edition of *Current Biography*. The entire compilation of the Hall Johnson arrangements for *The Green Pastures* can be found in the book entitled *Green Pastures Spirituals.*

Connelly, Marc. *The Green Pastures*. New York: Farrah and Rinehart, 1929.

Current Biography. 1945. New York: H.W. Wilson Co., 1945.

Johnson, Hall. *The Green Pastures Spirituals*. New York: Farrah and Rinehart, 1930.

Lovell, John. *Black Song: The Forge and the Flame.* New York: The MacMillan Company, 1972.

Southern, Eileen, *The Music of Black Americans, A History.* New York: W.W. Norton and Company, 1971

LUCIUS HENRY HOLSEY

Cade, John. *Holsey—The Incomparable.* New York: Pageant Press, n.d.

The Christian Index. September 9,1920.

Holsey, Lucius Henry. *Autobiography, Sermons, Speeches and Essays.* Atlanta: S.L. Holsey, Printer, 1899.

Holsey, Lucius Henry. "The Race Problem." *Atlanta Constitution*, 1900.

Knox Institute Catalogue.

New York Independent. December 16,1897.

Paine College Catalogue. 1915-16.

Paine College, *Sixty Years of Progress/Paine College.* Augusta, Ga.: The College [between 1926 and 1932].

THE BLACK JOURNALISTS

Copies of three of the early twentieth century black newspapers listed in this chapter are on file in the Special Collections department at the University of Georgia Library.

Athens Blade. October 31,1879 and February 20,1880.

Athns Clipper. August 31,1901. *Colored American.* January 16, 1904.

Athens Daily Herald. Special edition, 1914.

Athens Georgian. November 7,1876.

Athens Voice. June 12,1975.

Athens Voice. April 1980 and July 29, 1980.

The Bright Side of African Life, Philadelphia: A.M.E. Publishing House, 1898.

Dann, M.E. *The Black Press 1827-1890.*

Heard, W.H. *From Slavery to the Bishopric in the A.M.E. Church.* New York: New York Times Press, 1969.

Meier, August. *Negro Thought in America 1880-1915.* Ann Arbor: University of Michigan Press, 1963.

Rawick, George P., ed. *The American Slave.* Georgia Narratives Parts 1 & 2. Vol. 12. Westport, Conn: Greenwood Publishing Co., 1972.

Republique, November 3, 1923.Walton Jr, Hanes. *Black Republicans: The Politics of the Black and Tans.* Metuchen, New Jersey: Scarecrow Press, 1975.

PICTURE CREDITS

Book Cover: D.L. Earnest Collection, Hargrett Rare Book and Manuscript Library, University of Georgia

Introduction to the Third Edition: xv Daniel Borremans

Jubilee: Opposite page 1 Drawing by Don Smith.

Two Lawmakers: 24 Al Hester; 36 Keith Heard.

The Black Church: 38 Alice Wimberly; 43, 48 Phelps-Stokes Studies.

Educators and Their Schools: 52, 58 (bottom), 66, Special Collections, University of Georgia Library; 62 (bottom) *Athens Daily Herald*; 58 (top), 62 (top), 64 *Era of Promise and Progress*; 69, 72, 74, 75, 79 Phelps-Stokes Studies; 81 Conoly Hester; 87 Kim Callaway; 89 Donarell Green IV.

Who Are We?: 97, 99, 101, 103 D.L. Earnest Collection, University of Georgia Library; 107 Photo by Richard Fowlkes; 105 Dr. Donarell Green; 109 Hattie Jackson; 111 Photo by Bob Simonton; 113 Clarke County School District.

Samuel F. Harris: 114, 122, 125 Black Mammy Memorial Institute Brochure; 120 *Who's Who in Colored America*.

Medical Pioneers: 130, Alice Wimberly; 134, 140, 143 *Athens Daily Herald*; 141 Special Collections, University of Georgia Library; 146 Fred O. Smith; 157 Dr. Donarell Green; 147 Hiram Collection, University of Georgia Library.

Lucius Henry Holsey: 154, 162 *Autobiography, Sermons, Speeches and Essays: Sixty Years of Progress.*

Hall Johnson: 166 *Current Biography*, 1905; 172 *The Music of Black Americans.*

Black Journalists: 174 *The Colored American*; 184 *Athens Daily Herald*; 181, 187 Microfilm Collections, University of Georgia Library; 188 Fred Smith; 190 *The Bright Side of African Life.*

The *Athens Daily Herald* Special Sections 1871 and 1874, Phelps-Stokes Fellowship Studies, and the D. L. Earnest and Hiram collections are used courtesy of the Hargrett Rare Book and Manuscript Library, University of Georgia. Black Mammy Memorial Institute materials are in the Mildred Rutherford and James Reap collections, and are also published courtesy of Hargrett Rare Book and Manuscript Library, University of Georgia.

INDEX

C

D

E

H

K

L

R

CPSIA information can be obtained
at www.ICGtesting.com
Printed in the USA
BVHW071214050421
604207BV00007B/648